Supernatural Safety

Supernatural Safety:

A Paranormal DIY Guide

By Marlene Pardo Pellicer

All rights reserved worldwide under the Berne Convention. No parts of this book may be reproduced by any mechanical, photographic or electronic process or in the form of a phonographic recording; nor may it be stored in a retrieval system, transmitted or otherwise copied for public or private use other than as brief quotations embodied in articles and reviews, without prior written permission from the author.

SUPERNATURAL SAFETY: A PARANORMAL DIY GUIDE. Copyright © Marlene Pardo Pellicer. First Printing 2018. Printed in the United States of America

Notice: Although the author and publisher have made every effort to ensure that the information in this book was correct at press time, the author and publisher do not assume and hereby disclaim any liability to any party for any loss, damage, or disruption caused by errors or omissions, whether such errors or omissions result from negligence, accident, or any other cause.

First Edition:
First Printing

PUBLISHED BY ELEVENTH HOUR LLC
www.11thhour.company

PRINT ISBN 978-0-9991605-4-1
E-BOOK ISBN 978-0-9991605-5-8

If asked what I am most proud of, three words are always first. They are Adrienne, Brandon and Andrew the names of my children. They have been my teachers in understanding the depths of an over-trivialized sentiment called Love. They have also been the source of the most hair-raising and hair-pulling moments of my life as well. No wonder I appeared fearless in the face of the supernatural to my clients.

This book is dedicated to them, and so the journey continues…

Image Sources

Pixabay.com
Wikimedia Commons
Wikipedia
Images in the Public Domain

Cover Design - Eleventh Hour LLC

About The Author

Marlene is a native Miamian and the founder of Miami Ghost Chronicles, and she has been a paranormal investigator since the 1990s. She has worked mainly with research groups in Florida, but she has also assisted other organizations and private clients across the country.

She is the producer and host of the paranormal talk show, *Stories of the Supernatural* in which she interviews, authors, experts and any person who has witnessed the unexplained. She is also the narrator of the podcast show *Nightshade Diary* and the blog author of *Stranger Than Fiction Stories*. She appeared in S1E1 of *Paranormal Survivor* and S1 of *Haunted Hospitals.*

Marlene is a freelance writer who holds a Master of Science degree in Human Behavior & Health. She is a certified master hypnotist and considers herself a subconscious behaviorist. She has worked in the telecommunications field and as an investigator for a state-level agency (that shall remain unnamed).

Her books, *Haunted History of the Old West's Wicked Ladies & The Bad Hombres They Loved (2017)* and *The Lady in the Blue Kimono: Film Noir Murders (2018)* are available on her website and a fourth book, *An Odd Collection of Old & Obscure True Ghost Stories* will be coming out in 2019.

WWW.MIAMIGHOSTCHRONICLES.COM

WWW.STORIESOFTHESUPERNATURAL.INFO

WWW.MARLENEPARDO.COM

TABLE OF CONTENTS

- ❖ Foreword — 8
- ❖ Introduction — 10

1 - The Ground Rules — 12
2 - Everything But the Ghost — 15
3 - It is a Ghost, Now What? — 25
4 - Why Are They Haunting — 120
5 - Where the Rubber Meets the Road — 192
6 - When to Call In the Calvary — 199

- ❖ Sources — 205

FOREWORD

St. Michael, first champion of the kingship of Christ, pray for us! Glorious Prince of the heavenly hosts and victor over rebellious spirits, be mindful of me, I who am so weak and sinful, and yet so prone to pride and ambition. Lend me, I pray, your powerful aid in every temptation and difficulty, and above all do not forsake me in my last struggle with the powers of evil. Amen.

Brothers and Sisters, as an ordained exorcism-deliverance minister, and a survivor of several severe demonic attacks, I can assure you that demons are very real, and everywhere! Their hatred for us is off the charts, and there are no words to adequately describe that their very existence revolves around our demise, and the never-ending torture of our Souls. Whether you are a non-believer experiencing paranormal activity, a novice beginner, ghost hunter or a seasoned veteran paranormal investigator, we all need to stay humble, and be aware of the very real dangers in this field. Some mistakes can cost you your life or worse.

The person who came up with the saying, "I would rather rule in hell than serve in Heaven", is currently dog paddling in a sea of volcanic lava for eternity. Sounds like fun, huh?!

Once again, Marlene Pardo Pellicer has provided us all with must read material in a book that needs to be on every shelf, or better yet, in every paranormal equipment bag for out in the field problem solving!

And for Mom and Dad to browse through before telling the kids, "It is all in their imagination"…

Good luck and God bless,
Rev. Shawn Whittington
Host of Vegas Supernatural

Supernatural Safety

Introduction

These are the two questions I get the most as a paranormal investigator, "Do I have a ghost?", and "How do I get rid of the ghost in my house?"

These questions sound simple enough, but what follows depends mostly on whether there is a true haunting taking place. In the cases where there is actual supernatural activity present, how to handle it depends on what type of ghost you have.

Is it attached to the structure, to the land, to you? Is the activity benign, possibly residual, or is it malicious and sometimes even dangerous?

If you are fearful, which is always going to work against you, even the simplest manifestation is going to scare the pants off you. You might be in denial and have been putting off dealing with a maleficent occurrence in your home because you were just too scared thinking you did not know how to handle it.

Knowledge is power, and that is the first thing you need when handling a haunting. Next step is to throw out the stereotypes you see in movies and reality shows, because their goal is usually to make you scared, and that is not what you want.

Whatever turns out to be the reality of your situation, you have to believe that you have the right to be in the place you have chosen to live in. Whether you own, rent or live free with parents or friends, this is the first step towards empowering yourself. It will serve you well into the future if you ever find yourself in a similar situation.

Supernatural Safety

CHAPTER 1
THE GROUND RULES

The majority of times, your ghost was once a living human being. They might not be aware of you and are stuck going through a routine they followed for years, or they are reliving the last moments of their lives. They might not even understand that they are dead.

If they are aware of you, they might be trying to communicate either to find out why no one speaks to them, or for the very simple reason of telling you to get out of their house.

So that is why it is so important to identify the type of ghost or ghosts you have, why they are stuck and possibly what they want from you.

This is necessary because your approach is going to depend on the answers to those questions. The wrong method can end up with two results. The first is that nothing changes, or the worse outcome is that it ramps up activity. Those answers lay the groundwork for choosing what methods you want to employ, and more importantly, is whether you believe they will work. Belief is one of the most important ingredients if you want to be successful.

Before you make the first attempt in laying your spirit, you also need to get a clear picture if this ghost is unhappy or negative, or just friendly and wants to hang out with the living. This is not a one size fit all solution.

There is one scenario where you put on the brakes before implementing any effort to remove a ghost from your home yourself. If you have had plenty of instances where the manifestations are unquestionably negative, your best course of action is to contact a reputable paranormal group to verify what is truly going on in your home. We will go over ways of selecting the right group later on.

One Hollywood stereotype that you have to forget about is that a haunting can be resolved only after one try. If you think that everything will be taken care of with a clap of thunder, sprinkling holy water and poof it is over, think again.

Ghosts like most human beings are complicated, and so are the reasons why they haunt. Even more so is their reason for resisting going into the afterlife.

Throughout all the years, I have researched the paranormal I have seen the effect that living with an earthbound spirit can have on a person's life. Unquestionably, in the end it is works against the living person's best interests even if the entity is a family member or loved one.

Throughout the book, I will refer to ghosts and spirits. Ghosts are those that are earthbound by choice or circumstance, and spirits are those that have crossed over but decide to return occasionally for reasons that sometimes only they understand.

CHAPTER 2
EVERYTHING BUT THE GHOST

Thanks to the spate of paranormal reality shows, when someone hears a strange noise coming from the rafters, feels a cool wind blow down the hallway or an eerie sensation when visiting the basement, the first thought is that it is a ghost! In truth, this is usually the last thing that it is.

ELECTRICIAN VERSUS EXORCIST

Let us look at one of the most common occurrences that are blamed on ghosts. It is something as simple as flickering lights, appliances that act weird or burn out prematurely.

It might not be your first move, but your best bet is to call an electrician and have all the electrical connections checked out. There is not a best or worst-case scenario to this situation, and it is just different degrees of best. If everything checks out OK, first, the mystery of the flickering lights is solved one way or the other. Second, if you have faulty wiring you might have dodged the "house fire" bullet, and last, you know you can proceed with the ghost theory if it is determined it is not an electrical problem.

You might as well make good use of the electrician while he is there and ask him to test for high electro-magnetic fields (EMFs). High EMFs can be the culprit for feelings of being watched, getting goose pimples and even hallucinating. Different people get affected different ways and some of the weirdest feelings are not supernatural at all but just a product of high EMFs at the location. Have the electrician start with the electrical box and then out from there throughout the structure.

The reason to rule out high EMF readings is that it can affect your brain. It can cause dizziness, disorientation and nausea. It can produce feelings of uneasiness, paranoia, depression and even acute terror. These are the most common sensations that people describe in connection to a haunting but in reality are the product of high EMFs.

A call to the electrician should be your first option if you suspect you are haunted, and an exorcist should be the last.

FEATHERS, FUR AND FANGS

There is nothing scarier than waking up from a deep sleep and hearing something scratching behind the walls somewhere in the room you occupy, or the sound of something walking or running across the roof of your house.

I have had cases where occupants of a house have run out and slept in their car. They would not investigate until it is daytime, and of course, nothing is found, so even levelheaded adults start tossing the G word around.

When I have conducted a pre-interview with clients who describe these types of noises, I ask them if they have had anyone inspect their house for pests. I will get silence at the other end of the line, but there is a good reason for this question, because there is a chance it is an animal that is causing the noises. They will swear that on the contrary it is a ghost making its presence known. You would be surprised at the small spaces where an animal can crawl into.

They could go into these areas to escape inclement or cold weather, to breed, or if they are sick or hurt; sometimes they are stuck and cannot get out.

Chimneys are notorious for being the Motel 6 for birds and small animals. Let me tell you my own personal stories. Our house has a chimney that empties out into a small fireplace in the living room. We hung our flat screen TV above the mantelpiece, so you can imagine my surprise when one day I had a small owl staring at me from its perch off the edge of the television.

There was only one point of entry, which was the chimney. We opened our front door and shooed it out, but I laughed thinking that if it had flown up the staircase into the second story without being seen, I would probably have gone crazy trying to figure out what was making noises up there, considering it is unoccupied and used as office and storage space.

Another time, I was sitting in my office and kept hearing weird noises coming from somewhere in the first floor of the house. I would walk around and just stand in the middle of the house, all was quiet and I mean quiet. I was the only one in the house at that time. I would return to my office and within a few minutes, it would start again. Most disquieting of all is that I could not make head or tails of what type of noise it was.

The third time it started up even the dogs starting to whine and look around, so I knew they were hearing it as well.

On the Paranormal-O-Meter the needle was starting to climb. Alone in the house with inexplicable noises and your animals are reacting as well, the classic indicators of a ghostly visitor.

The last time I was standing in the living room, like before the noise had stopped. I scanned the room, and just happened to look at the empty fireplace. We have a concave screen over it that seals the opening. Guess what was staring at me from the recesses of the darkness? A blackbird! It would quiet down and just watch me when I walked into the room, and then flutter against the screen and try to get out when I left. I opened the front door, pulled back the screen and it made a b-line for the great outdoors.

It has happened a few more times especially in the summertime when the chimney is not in use. I have a pair of blackbirds that have made a nest right under the eaves of the roof, between the outer wall and an inner wall that is part of a closet. They return every spring.

One day I had a relative staying over for a few days and I forgot to mention this. I heard him come thundering down the staircase calling my name. His eyes were as big as saucers as he described hearing scratching coming from the closet. He was thinking that I had given him the haunted bedroom.

I smiled and told him it was just birds that had a nest between the walls. He did not laugh; he really thought I was trying to blame the noises on animals and it took some convincing to assure him there was nothing supernatural going on.

A version of this story plays out countless times, and unfortunately, many people do not try to figure out what is the real source of the disturbance because they are convinced it is paranormal in origin.

Rats, raccoons, opossums, pigeons, bats and down here in South Florida, huge snakes are just some of the animals that can decide to share living quarters with you. They are not human, but they are definitely not ghosts.

CREAKING DOORS AND COLD SPOTS

The hallmark of the traditional haunted house is a creaky door, or one that opens by itself. This is frequently described by people complaining that their house is haunted; however it could just be a door that is not hung right or sits on hinges that should be replaced. Cabinet doors can swing open inexplicably if the latches are worn out.

If you live in an older home it could have shifted, and a slant in the floor that you might not be aware of will cause a door to close slowly as if by unseen hands.

You might have an intrepid pet that has figured out how to open the door. I can vouch for this because my dogs know how to test the door to check if the latch has not caught, and they can push it open.

How about drafts or cold spots? Just like the creaky door, the cold spot is the traditional indicator of a ghostly presence, based on the belief that the entity is drawing energy from the environment in order to manifest.

This could be caused by a heating or cooling system that is starting to go bad, or openings around your doors or windows. It might be months or even years in the making until the day arrives when you really notice the difference in temperature, and it is not as sudden as you might initially think. It could be as simple as someone that changed the slant on a vent.

I had a case where the family was complaining that they would feel a cool draft that would come down a short hallway leading to a bathroom and bedroom. I asked them when they had started to experience this. It turned out they had moved a large china cabinet that had stood at a wall at the end of that hallway for years. That piece of furniture in essence had blocked chinks in the wall, and not allowed the draft to be felt. Once it was gone, voilà, a cold spot seemed to have developed overnight.

Bad plumbing can cause thumping behind walls or what sounds like footsteps.

Whatever you are experiencing, you should rule out the regular explanation for it. You might feel a little foolish if it turns out to be something mundane, but this is what you should really be hoping for all along. The solution can be as simple as a DIY project or just hiring a handyman.

If you are renting, omit the part about thinking it is haunted if you want your landlord to send someone over to check plumbing, electricity or doors, as they might think you are trying to get out of a lease or not paying your rent.

I have mentioned only a few of the most regularly described incidents that people attribute to a haunting. You might be experiencing a version similar to what is been described, or something very different. The point being made is that before you jump to the conclusion that it is paranormal, despite what might appear to be an inexplicable incident, allow for the possibility that it might have nothing to do with a ghost.

This approach offers you something that is priceless; it is called peace of mind.

CHAPTER 3
It Is A Ghost, Now What?

Let us say you have ruled out all the non-paranormal reasons for what is happening in your home, what is your next step? Your approach is going to depend on what or who is in your home.

A Ship In The Night

These spirits are not bound to a place, and might be making an appearance either because of the location or because of someone living there. It might be an anniversary, if someone in the house is experiencing a crisis or if it has been summoned. These entities understand fully that they are dead, and their intent is never to scare or harm the living. You might only smell a certain scent that is associated with them, or they manifest some type of object that has special significance for them or the person it is intended for. This spirit might appear once and never again.

The spirits of the recently deceased also fall into this category. They are saying a last good-bye to reassure their loved ones that they are OK now. They might just come in dreamtime. Some spirits have gone back to where they once lived or worked at, almost like a nostalgia tour, and then they are gone.

This type of spirit is handled in one of two ways. If you do not know who it is or what it is about, just ignore it and wish them to rest in peace. Do not give it your attention, and much less your fear, and within a few hours or days it is gone.

If it is someone you know the approach is very similar. Just as they are letting you know they are OK, you need to let them know you are good as well. If this is a recent death and you are grieving, this might take a lot of courage on your part, but you do not want them to stay behind in order to comfort you.

RESIDUAL

This type of haunting could be a full-body apparition, a smell, sounds, manifested individually or all together. This could occur only at a certain part of the house or the land, or at a certain time, daily or an anniversary.

Many battlefield scenes are just a residual haunting; there is no intelligence, there is no trapped soul.

The reason for this type of haunting is an activity that was done repetitively for many years, or an instant of extreme fear and anger that imprints itself on the fabric of the place.

This is why you will have residual ghosts going through doors that are no longer there, or are seen walking on a floor level that does not exist anymore. They are not aware of the living and do not try to interact with you.

A case I was involved in had the smell of baking bread and brewing coffee waft throughout a two-story house three to four times a week always in the morning. Then it would stop for months and return. This house was over 100 years old, and no doubt, this activity was done countless times throughout the years.

Another case turned out to have the sound of someone walking up and down stairs that did not exist anymore. Again, this was an older house where they had a servant's staircase at one time in the back of the house. During a remodeling of the house, these stairs had been removed, but no doubt these stairs were used innumerable times throughout the years, and not surprisingly the steps would be heard always during the daytime, which would have been the busiest time in a household which used a full staff of servants.

The phenomena attached to a residual haunting are usually the easiest for different people to witness.

Another trigger for certain residual haunting is the weather. It does not have to be stormy; it could just be conditions that mimic very closely what it was like the day of the event that has imprinted itself in the fabric of that place.

Suppose you are experiencing a residual haunting of a disturbing image such as a wounded soldier. You could tell yourself, it is not really a ghost and just something like a hologram, but let us face it you still do not want to have this anywhere in your house.

This is one of those situations where this will fade with time. You have to start by smudging with a sage stick maybe once a month. Depending on your religious belief, you can ask an intelligent spirit, God, angels; whatever you feel is appropriate to cleanse the area of all these residual energies. It is almost like stripping away layers of wallpaper. It will take more than once, however before you know it the manifestation will start to fade and eventually disappear.

A residual haunting can be an uncomfortable feeling you get when you go to a certain room or part of the house. It could be feelings of dread, anxiety, fear and sometimes an actual physical symptom. This could be due to picking up empathically on the intense feelings experienced at certain times in that particular place. Sometimes you know the history of the place, however even if you do not know, remember human drama plays out behind closed doors and no one outside the place is none the wiser, and much less able to document what happened there.

There are people who unknowingly occupy what used to be a "sick room" for prior occupants of a house. They will notice feeling ill only when they are in that room. They will see their physicians who give them a clean bill of health. Sometimes it takes month before they realize that it is only when they are in that particular space that they develop certain physical and/or mental symptoms. This is a type of residual haunting.

A DIFFERENT REALITY

There are ghosts, sometimes residual but many times intelligent, which are oblivious to the living; they have no desire to be seen or interact with humans. They are invisible ghosts, and most of the times they are caught only with a camera. They are hardly ever seen with the naked eye; many of the famous "ghost pictures" fall into this category.

The Madonna of Bachelors Grove Cemetery in Chicago, The Tulip Staircase Ghost photographed at the Queen's House at the National Maritime Museum in Greenwich, England, The Ghost Boy picture taken inside the Amityville House thought to be John Defeo; are just to name a few.

For the few well-known photographs there are hundreds taken by average people that are never publicized. The photos are taken by persons who are trying to capture the image of a landscape, a building a group of people, anything but what shows up on the film.

These "invisible ghosts" are sometimes captured once and other times periodically throughout the years.

I myself have never captured a clear-cut picture of what is recognizably a human or animal figure, however I have caught strange anomalies and mists that I know were not seen with the naked eye when the photograph was taken.

Brown Lady of Raynham Hall c.1936
Source - Wikipedia

Supernatural Safety
33

THE STORY OF THE BROWN LADY

The ghost story of the Brown Lady of Raynham Hall would have remained a little known story if it were not for a photograph taken by Captain Hubert C. Provand on September 19, 1936. *Country Life* magazine was about to publish an article about Raynham Hall and he along with his assistant Indre Shira were taking photographs of the estate, when they captured a semitransparent figure on the staircase, a favorite haunt of the Brown Lady.

The photograph was not the first time this enigmatic and tragic ghost had been sighted. The apparition was said to be Lady Dorothy Walpole (1686-1726). This is her story.

She had fallen in love with the Second Viscount Townshend, but her father who was his guardian did not approve of the match. He went on to marry another, but became a widower in 1711.

Unbeknownst to Charles Townshend in those intervening years Dorothy Walpole had become the mistress of Lord Wharton (1648-1715), a well-known rake and libertine who was almost forty years her senior. He was known as a debaucher of young ladies.

In 1673, before Dorothy Walpole was even born, Wharton married Ann, niece of the notorious Duke of Rochester who tried to stop the marriage due to Wharton's reputation. Anne was bookish and innocent, and died a miserable death in her mid-twenties from syphilis she had contracted from her husband.

Wharton then went on to marry Lucy Loftus, who was known to help her husband seduce young girls. Both of them were flagrantly unfaithful to each other. It was no surprise that their son Philip was the founder of the Hellfire club.

The story goes that Townshend was in ignorance of this affair and married Dorothy shortly after the death of his first wife. It turned out their marriage was an unhappy one.

Dorothy was known as a frivolous creature with a weakness for expensive, pretty clothing. However, she loved something even more, which were her children. They were kept from her, and their upbringing was left in the hands of their paternal grandmother at Raynham Hall. Dorothy bore her husband seven children from 1714 to 1724. He already had five children by his first wife, Elizabeth Pelham.

Whether Dorothy's affair with Wharton was true or only rumor, it might have served to cause strife between her and her husband. Perhaps Dorothy loved her children, but preferred spending her time in London, and at court enjoying the privileges extended to a noblewoman of that age.

Whether Dorothy's daily existence was marred by separation from her children, or if she lived a life of carefree indulgence, it was cut short at the age of forty when she died from smallpox. There were rumors that circulated, one that she had died from a broken neck after falling or being pushed down the grand staircase at Raynham Hall. Another story is that her death in 1726 was staged and that she was kept imprisoned for many years afterwards in Raynham Hall. The wandering spirit is said to be looking for her children.

During those intervening years, the family would let Raynham Hall out for years; perhaps the Brown Lady was already making her presence known.

> RAYNHAM HALL, Norfolk.—To be LET, for a term of years, with early possession, RAYNHAM HALL and PARK, together with the right of Sporting over about 13,000 acres of land. The House is furnished and fit for the reception of a family of distinction.—Particulars may be had at the Offices of Messrs. Blake, White, Ainge, and Blake, 14, Essex-street, London; and of Mr. Overton, Fakenham.

AD THAT APPEARED IN THE *MORNING CHRONICLE* (LONDON), JANUARY 12, 1825

In 1836, Sir Charles and Lady Townshend had come to Raynham Hall upon the completion of a remodeling job. Captain Frederick Marryat was their neighbor and along with other guests had been invited to spend a few days there. To their dismay, stories started to circulate that the house was haunted and several of their guests made excuses to leave early. Servants also quit, claiming that the apparition of a lady wearing a brown dress with yellow trim had been sighted in different parts of Raynham Hall.

The baronet told Captain Marryat of his predicament and being magistrate of the county he asked to stay in the "haunted room", suspecting that it was smugglers who had circulated the story in order to drive occupants from the house.

There was a portrait of Lady Dorothy hung in the room where he was staying. Captain Marryat slept with a loaded revolver under his pillow, whether it was to shoot at the phantom or smugglers remains unknown.

On the third night he was at Raynham Hall, he accompanied two of Townshend's nephews to their room to see a firearm. It was late and they both accompanied him back to his room. As they made their way back down the dark corridor, they saw the glimmer of a lamp coming towards them from the other end. All three men thought it was one of the ladies coming to visit the nursery. Being in a state of undress, the men stepped into one of the empty rooms that lined the corridor and watched through a chink between the double doors as the light come nearer.

The figure stopped before the door where Captain Marryat stood on the other side. Cold sweat poured from him as he recognized the figure as the same one whose portrait hung in the room where he was staying. He already had his finger on the revolver that he had taken with him, when the apparition raised the lamp to her face and "grinned maliciously and diabolically at him". There was no doubt that this was no smuggler, and Captain Marryat sprang into the hallway and discharged his weapon aimed at the ghost's face. The figure instantly disappeared and the three men who had seen her, now stood in an empty corridor. The bullet had gone through the door of the room opposite and lodged in one of the panels. Captain Marryat left Raynham Hall that same day.

It was Christmas of 1849, and the family gathered at Raynham Hall. One of those attending was Major Loftus and his wife who were relatives of the Townshends. Early one morning after finishing an all night card game he was making his way back to his room with a companion, who pointed to a lady wearing a brown, silk gown standing on the landing. He called out to the unknown lady who promptly disappeared. The next day he waited for her to appear, and she did not disappoint him. This time he got a better look at her, and described her as a handsome woman, but where her eyes should have been were two empty sockets.

Major Loftus told his story to the other guests the following day and they all stayed up to see if she made a third appearance but she did not. What did happen though was that the entire staff of servants gave notice.

Lord Charles Townshend became infuriated and suspected there was some trickery afoot. He hired detectives to masquerade themselves as servants in order to entrap the person to blame for the phantom. They stayed there for months, without a sighting of the Brown Lady or finding a live person as the perpetrator of the distasteful joke.

The next report of the Brown Lady came in 1926 when Lady Townshend's young son George and an American friend who was visiting met a lady dressed in brown on the stairs. She frightened them especially when they realized they could see the stairs through her.

In the 1930s, she was seen by Mrs. Cyril Fitzroy and her daughter who were visiting Raynham Hall.

The next sighting of the Brown Lady was the famous photo taken in 1936.

In 1938, the current Viscountess Townshend in a newspaper interview confirmed the story of the Brown Lady and other phantoms as well that haunted Raynham

Hall. She explained that the story that Lady Dorothy had been imprisoned and starved to death was false. The circumstances would have made it impossible, and the fact that she was the sister of the powerful Sir Robert Walpole would not have allowed her disappearance to go unnoticed.

She said there was a ghost of a duke known as the Red Cavalier who haunted the Monmouth Room.

The third ghost was that of a child seen by Lady Townshend's own governess, who saw Lady Norah Bentinck arrive with three children for a visit at Raynham Hall. She was surprised at this, as she had heard that Lady Norah only had two children. When she asked after the third child, they told her that they had only brought two children. The governess described a little girl dressed in a picture frock that accompanied the other children up the steps and then ran through the hall into the Stone Parlor.

Many skeptics have tried to debunk the 1936 picture of the Brown Lady; however, no one can explain why a famous and well-known photographer would have a need to create the illusion of the transparent image caught in the photograph.

ARTIST'S RENDITION OF THE BROWN LADY
BASED ON LADY TOWNSHEND'S INTERVIEW C.1938
SOURCE - WINNIPEG TRIBUNE

LADY DOROTHY TOWNSHEND NEE WALPOLE
THE BROWN LADY OF RAYNHAM HALL

to create the illusion of the transparent image caught in the photograph.

ARTIST'S RENDITION OF THE BROWN LADY
BASED ON LADY TOWNSHEND'S INTERVIEW C.1938
SOURCE - WINNIPEG TRIBUNE

LADY DOROTHY TOWNSHEND NEE WALPOLE
THE BROWN LADY OF RAYNHAM HALL

Supernatural Safety

THE MIST

These ghosts can never be mistaken for a regular person because you can see through them. They are semi-transparent and in some cases, you can actually see some type of detail, other times it is just a human-sized mist that will float or dart away.

These misty phantoms could be residual, but they could be intelligent especially if it moves away from you and makes an effort not to be seen.

I myself had an experience when I was on an investigation. I was sitting down on the floor with my back against the wall. It was after midnight, and I was keeping an eye on two rooms that opened off the same hallway at the top of a staircase. I was periodically taking temperature readings and I had a digital recorder running. I purposely had brought the lights down low, and I was the only team member upstairs.

My mind was wandering a little, and we had been at the house already for a few hours. Suddenly I had the distinct feeling of being watched. I also smelled the faint odor of ionization, like right before a thunderstorm. This was very unusual considering I was indoors and the weather outside was clear.

The actual room I was sitting in was almost empty, and only had a bed frame with a headboard propped up against the furthest wall.

I checked the temperature, there was no significant change and when I looked in the corner furthest from me, I saw what could only be described as the darkness shifting. I squinted and saw a misty, vaguely human-size figure taking form.

I looked down for just a moment to make sure my recorder was still going and then the most amazing thing happened. The misty figure made a movement as if it had actually become aware of me, which made me are turned in such a way that you only see the curve of their face or their jaw line.

Some are seen to move in slow motion, as if they were underwater, including the way their hair moves. They could appear this way even if they did not die in any way connected to water.

Some of these ghosts are seen in their death state that can be quite horrendous. If you recall a scene from the movie *The Sixth Sense,* towards the end when the character Cole Sear sees the ghost of a woman just killed in a biking accident looking at him through the car window. Her face is bloody and she has no expression on her face. That is a dead giveaway (no pun intended).

Others appear in the clothing they were buried in especially if it held a special significance such as a wedding dress or a uniform.

I participated in a case several years ago in which the family was experiencing a haunting in which their children's toys were being manipulated. They had wonder later on if this is what I had felt watching me earlier.

It darted very quickly into a closet that had a partially open door.

I quickly got up and inspected the closet, and of course, it was empty, just like both rooms. The faint "it is about to rain" smell had also dissipated.

MISTAKEN FOR HUMAN

These ghosts are solid and are frequently mistaken for a living person. They are seen at night and during the day. If they are in period clothes, they are thought to be reenactors, tour guides or docents. One of the giveaways that they are not a living human being is that they have an unblinking, expressionless look on their face that no living person can imitate. It can be very disquieting. Another clue is that you really cannot see their face clearly. They have their back to you, or they several small children, and especially the toys that were left in the family room area would be moved, and the parents would hear this going on when they had retired for the night.

Later on, it turned out that this was the spirit of a neighbor boy who had been hit by a vehicle outside their home. He had been buried in his first communion clothing, and this is how he had been seen a few times by the family. What was unusual about this case was that this event occurred right before they moved out of the state and came down to Florida. This child spirit traveled down with them, attracted by the happy family-like atmosphere the home had, as well as some confusion of the death state, which can happen with young children when they pass away suddenly.

The child was successfully crossed over to the other side and the activity surrounding the toys stopped.

THUMBING A RIDE INTO ETERNITY

Hitchhiking ghosts are a staple of urban myths in just about every part of the United States. Most of them follow the formula retold in one of the most famous version, which is Chicago's Resurrection Mary. The story starts when a woman is seen walking by the side of a road and when she is taken to her destination, whether it is a cemetery or a home, she disappears from the vehicle.

In some versions the driver knocks at the door of the house the hitchhiker directed them to before she vanished, and he is told that the girl in question died many years before in a car accident.

There are hitchhiking ghosts that are tied into grisly crimes, and which are probably stuck in a loop reliving their last moments. In the United States, hitchhiking became popular during the Depression, even though both those picking up hitchhikers, and the hitchhikers themselves could be robbed, sexually assaulted or even killed.

During the 1960s into the 1970s is when young women would hitchhike and disappear or become victims of unspeakable crimes. An example of this is the Santa Rosa Hitchhiker Murders that occurred from 1972 to 1973, when at least seven women were killed by an unknown assailant. The crimes have never been solved.

There are stories of ghostly hitchhikers, usually described as young women standing on the edge of the road after dark. Once the drivers get a good look at her, she is either faceless or horribly disfigured. It is believed these are the ghosts of hitchhikers that have been killed while they were thumbing a ride.

My own personal story about a similar phantom to these was not a result of an investigation, but was retold to me by a good friend of mine named Eddie. He was returning home to Miami via U.S. 27, (AKA Bloody 27 due to the amount of fatalities on it), which is a long, unlit road that traverses through the middle of Florida, passing through small towns, but mostly sugarcane fields.

He was traveling with his wife late at night when he saw a tall man walking along the inside shoulder of the road. He pulled up ahead of him, deciding to give him a ride since you could walk for miles before getting to a gas station if your car had broken down. This was the 1980s, prior to the popularity of cellular phones.

He exited the vehicle and walked towards the man, who he said did not acknowledge him by calling out, waving or walking faster. He said that as he got closer to him he observed that the man looked very bedraggled, had dark cavernous eyes and kept walking with the same, slow tread. He said that a very bad feeling of dread overcame him and he retreated, got in his car and sped off.

Later he realized that he had not seen any car pulled over on the side as if it had broken down, which could have belonged to a stranded motorist.

Eddie was a large guy, an ex-police officer and in his twenties. He did not scare easy, and he admitted to me that he felt that he needed to get out of there quickly, and that there was something very unearthly taking place.

I have traveled this way many times at night and it is a lonely stretch of road, so back in those years it would have been very easy to spot a disabled car on the median of the road. It is a two-lane highway with no tolls, which makes it a favorite of long-distance truckers. The towns that dot the landscape are scarcely populated. The point is that this is not a place anyone takes a stroll through in the middle of the night, not even during the day.

So who was the tall man? He could have been anybody, but the area that is so desolate has a long history of being a dumpsite for bodies.

FURIOUS GHOSTS

These are the ghosts that I usually recommend an intervention from a paranormal group versus a DIY approach.

These unquiet souls find no peace because they are seeking either revenge or some type of justice that has been denied to them in regards to how they lost their life.

They are violent in their haunting, destructive and as time goes by they could be downright dangerous. The reason for this is that they are fueled by fury; never a good emotion in the living or the dead.

They could have been a murder victim that was made to look like a suicide, or their assailants were never arrested or convicted, and the worse, those that were killed and buried in secret. Perhaps no one including their family ever found out what happened to them, or where their body was buried or disposed of.

The circumstances of their deaths is not the only factor in this type of haunting, it also has to do with the personality they had when they were living. Many times, they were combative or had little or no belief in the afterlife. To them this is the only way to set the record straight, or to get vengeance for a wrong committed against them.

Your best bet is to not only get a qualified paranormal team, but also one that has a medium available. By this, I mean not someone who will do a blessing or smudge down the house. I mean a medium, someone who can communicate with the dead. Not all psychics are mediums.

Once you have worked in the paranormal field for some time, you realize how some ghosts only want to tell someone what happened to them, or just to be acknowledged and then that is it. It is over! They have gone on.

However to make sure you can convince those that have dug their heels in, you need a medium to bring them up to speed about the reality of their existence. As in they are dead, and possibly their family and even the person who did them wrong has long since passed on.

THE TROJAN HORSE

This is a type of haunting that involves malevolent ghosts that disguise themselves as something else, usually a child. Why? Because most human beings do not feel threatened by a child and want to help it.

I can imagine you are asking yourself, well what if it is really a child. Then pray for them, wish them peace AND ask for a parent or loved one to come get them.

Yes, it is that simple, and will probably have to be done various times.

Children usually have little reason to distrust, and when a parent comes to get them, they go quickly into the light, even if they have been lost for many years. Sometimes this child spirit does not understand that it is dead and they are looking for their family. If you suspect that this child did not have good parents, then ask the most appropriate person to come get them, or an angel to cross them over.

I cannot stress the caution that should be taken when handling this type of discarnate. Before you attempt direct communication do as I suggested especially if your own child is describing seeing or communicating with this child spirit. Do not encourage a relationship with a spirit and your child. The possible outcomes of this scenario can be disastrous.

One, this spirit might decide to attach to your child, in other words obsess or possess your child.

Two, it could try to convince your child to do something dangerous and make them a ghost as well. Even though in my experience this is usually not a child spirit but a non-human entity, which is trying to bring agony into the life of the humans living there by taking away their child.

Three, you could be dealing with a perversion of a child spirit who wants one of the adults to become their parent. Perhaps this child in life received little affection, and hungers for it and will stop at nothing to secure this attention and love. It will see other children or even adults as a rival for the caretaker they yearn for. It could be either parent, but this scenario usually involves a mother figure.

Ultimately, a true child spirit deserves to be in the presence of the Divine and not be trapped on this plane.

Of all these scenarios, the most problematic are those that I call the Trojan Horse; an entity that has disguised itself as a child to gain sympathy and acceptance.

This type of manipulation is not usually seen in a human ghost, but in a non-human entity that has a good understanding of human nature and what our weaknesses are.

Remember communication in any form with this type of entity is a slippery slope downward. You are extending an invitation, and then throwing the door wide open. You could argue that the ghost was already there before you moved in, but the invitation is not to the physical space, but the metaphysical space that surrounds you and where you live. You are opening your mind, your emotions and possibly all of your regular senses.

Until this day, a case where any type of activity is described as childlike sets off my alarm bells.

I have lost count of the cases that describe a very innocuous beginning, usually where the living think they are dealing with a child, eventually evolving into something much darker.

By the time, you realize there is no child spirit involved you could be earlobe deep in a serious and destructive haunting. This is absolutely not a DIY situation. You need to bring in a competent paranormal group who has experience in dealing with demonic forces.

My recommendation is that none of the team actually performs any rituals, but has access to a deliverance minister or a priest who can come in and handle it. The person could also be a shaman, a pagan, just about anyone who is well versed in dealing with non-human entities, and knows how to dislodge them. Make sure this person has actual experience, not just having read a book.

The reason for this recommendation is that the wrong person brought in will be chased out by the entity, and activity will get much worse.

DANGEROUS SYMPATHY

This involves objects. Even though this falls into the DIY category, do not pooh-pooh the caution that is needed with this type of situation. Nowadays it is very common to buy items at thrift stores, flea markets, garage sales or even pick them up from the curbside.

Before you bring it into your home, I suggest you do something that resounds with you on a spiritual or religious level. This could be saying a prayer, smudging it with sage, sprinkling it with holy water or imagining a white cleansing light around it. Again, this has to be something that you believe in.

I want to clarify that this precaution not only pertains to household objects, but to clothing or personal items.

Even if you do not get bad vibes, or know the history to the item, this step should be on your to-do list before bringing it into your home.

This is just a little insurance to make sure you do not import into your living space an item that has an attachment from someone who used it constantly, or felt ownership of this object.

If not the actual spirit of the person who used it, you could experience their thoughts and emotions, especially if they were intense.

Anxiety, fear even depression can be transmitted via an object that has been imprinted. This includes the symptoms of certain illnesses.

The experience I had with this type of situation came through helping out a family member who had bought a house that was in probate. It was a small, two-bedroom house that had been built in the 1940s. Very little had been done to change the house throughout the years, and later on it was found out that it had only had two owners.

On the top shelf of one of the closets, they had found a ballerina music box. From the flower pattern on the outside it looked like it had been manufactured during the 1970s, and it was in great shape. It was given to the family's eleven-year-old daughter who was going to occupy the room. She placed it on a nightstand next to where she slept.

About six months after they had moved in I got a call from my family members asking me to come over. They asked me not to say anything to anyone else in the family. I thought this request was very mysterious.

When I got there, it turned out the child occupying the room had started to have horrific nightmares shortly after moving in. The dreams were non-specific and vague but she felt a lot of fear. They had decided to call me when they noticed their daughter was starting to grow anxious when it was twilight, and she knew that soon she would be going to bed.

Believe me, by the time they contacted me they had gone through a whole checklist of what could be causing the nightmares and the only thing that was evident was that it had started after moving in. The parents were at their wits end. The child was the only person in the household who was having this experience.

They did not know the history of the house, only that it had been vacant for about a year before they moved in.

Besides the child's behavior, there was no other indication of a ghostly presence or haunting based on the answers they gave to my questions. I did not show up with a team or equipment but after years of doing this, there is an internal ting-aling-aling that goes off when you are in the presence of something paranormal. This was absent.

I went outside to see if I could feel anything. About two properties over, I caught sight of an old man watering his garden. I knew this could be a great source of information.

I went over to where he was and introduced myself (omitting the part about being a paranormal investigator). I asked him if he had lived in the house long, and he said yes. I made small talk and complimented him on his fruit trees, and then I asked him if he knew anything about the house I had just come from.

I hit pay dirt because he had lived in the neighborhood for over thirty years. He filled in all the blanks about the property. He told me that when he moved into the neighborhood a woman lived there by herself. She had little or no visitors and he never saw any family visit. He did not know how long she had been living there before he moved into his house. She was not friendly and did not talk to any of her neighbors.

He said that as the years went by she left her house less and less. She had been found dead inside the home a couple of years before. She had been deceased for about three days before she was discovered. Since she was rarely outside the house the neighbors did not catch on that she had died.

It was the mailman who smelled a horrible odor coming from the home when he put letters in the mailbox that was placed right next to the front door. Otherwise who knows how long she would have lain in her house undiscovered.

The neighbor told me the house had been full of items, and I gathered it was not clear if she had been a hoarder or if due to her advanced age, she had been quite elderly when she died, she had been unable to throw the items out.

Later on, I verified that the house had been mostly empty when my family members had inspected it. I asked them if they had found or kept anything that was there, and initially they said no until they realized that the music box had been found in the closet.

We guessed that since it had been in a top shelf towards the back of the closet it had been overlooked when the house was cleaned out.

I told my family about my suspicions and I said we could prove my theory by just removing the item from the house, and waiting to see what happened.

Their daughter was not given the real reason why it was removed. I took it with me, not to my house, but stashed it somewhere it could be retrieved if it turned out this was not the culprit.

Guess what, no more nightmares! Without knowing the particulars, I can only think that this child had this experience due to her proximity to what had been the property of a person who might have been a hoarder in life. She might have also suffered from senility and dementia. These qualities had been imprinted on the one remaining item in the house, a music box she might have kept for more than thirty years.

My last piece of advice concerning used items is that if you ever feel intuition giving you a nudge to stay away from an item, leave it behind. I do not care if it has a great price or is in great shape.

THIS IS MY PLACE

These ghosts become more active when renovations take place. Make no mistake, remodeling does not start a haunting, the ghost has been there all along.

When work starts right after moving in, maybe the ghost is not upset about the renovations; they just do not want you and your family there.

Almost no investigations I have been involved in regarding complaints that activity started with renovations are accurate. If the family has already been living there, they will admit that they have been experiencing activity for quite some time that just became more intense after the work started.

It is during this part of an interview that I ask the magic question: Have you felt more stressed after renovations started? Invariably, the answer is yes. I have found that there is a perfect correlation with increased stress levels by the occupants of a home, with increased paranormal activity to go with it.

How about construction workers or handymen who are working in an empty house? It might be a residual haunting, and if you are working in an empty place how can you fail to hear strange noises? If it is an intelligent haunting, the entities are making their presence known not due to the work being done there, but because they are curious, or are claiming their territory against someone who they see as an intruder.

Sometimes entities try to chase people away because they have hidden something they think is valuable either in the home, possibly behind a wall or hidden room. Less than a hundred years ago many people did not trust banks, or lived too far from one and would stash, money, jewelry and important paperwork in their homes or bury it close by.

When floors and walls are being torn up, they fear that their "treasure" will be discovered. Sometimes it is not something valuable but something shameful they hid away. It could have been something that they stole, or something that could have been used against them lawfully or morally.

In some cases, a haunting is tied to the land, perhaps to a structure that existed there before. However, I have found that paranormal activity that covers an area is usually tied into a forgotten cemetery.

This could be a graveyard where not all the bodies were moved if a decision was made at some point to relocate the burials. In some cases, it was a family graveyard. There were areas sometimes that were used to bury indigents or undesirable that did not even get the benefit of a headstone, making it just much easier to forget what that land was once used for.

The remedy to this situation starts with attitude. The right attitude is that this is your home and your space. Just think what you would do if a stranger walked into your home. You would immediately claim ownership and order them out.

You could then have a conversation with the ghost, and nicely tell them that this is now your home and you will take good care of it, and then of course the part you never leave out when talking to a non-living human. It goes like this, "In case you did not know, you are dead." This might seem to be an overstatement, but not really. There are many ghosts who are not aware of this, or sometimes they have forgotten. Stating this makes it obvious why you do not want them there.

I would like to clarify that when I say have a conversation with the ghost, I mean doing something that you think makes you look foolish; like talking to thin air. There is no need for a Ouija board or any other instrument to communicate. In essence, you are just making an announcement.

Think of when someone uses a megaphone to say something so that everyone can hear. It is an FYI situation.

Go through the steps of clearing the space. It will take more than once. If it is tied to the land, it will move off to the surrounding areas, just like when you light a citronella candle and the mosquitoes disappear.

BONEYARDS

There are many investigators who claim that cemeteries are not haunted, because if a person were a ghost they would not stay in the cemetery but return home.

I beg to differ! You will find at least three types of haunting that take place anywhere human beings are buried.

The first is the confused human who does not understand that they are dead. After death, they see their body, but no matter how hard they try, they cannot reenter their body. You would think that seeing your body would be a good convincer that you are not among the living, but if you died traumatically, suddenly, under the influence of narcotics, during a surgery you might be in denial.

Yes, humans are good about denying the obvious, especially their own death. Sometimes they feel they have left something undone, they were too young or fear of punishment in the afterlife. Another segment that really does not want to accept the death state are those that thought that your consciousness ends when the body dies.

So what do these ghosts do? They follow their bodies around, from scene of death, to medical examiner to funeral home and then to the cemetery.

Once there, they are at a loss of what to do, but again they are fixated on being close to their body because they still retain their self-awareness. They see their ethereal body just how it looked when it was encased in a skin suit.

Once at the cemetery, depending on the personality of the entity and their state of mind when they died, they are either aware of the other ghosts or they are totally oblivious to them.

Time for these ghosts is not the same as when they were alive. They are not happy, but sometimes they interact with other dead, or they see funerals taking place or families visiting graves. They wander aimlessly around where their body was interred, and every once in a while they are captured on photographs or films, or even seen with the naked eye. They are like children staring through the window of a candy store. What they want the most is impossible, so they stay watching and hoping someone will help them understand what happened to them.

Many times those that are in mourning and visit a cemetery will experience a brush with one of these entities, and make the mistake of thinking it is their loved ones, and it is not.

There are occasions when these souls understand what happened to them at some point, and they leave this plane and cross over to where they should have gone originally, but others do not.

Do you think it is coincidental that necromancers steal bones from graveyards? Human bones can be bought legally, but guess what, those bones are usually devoid of any human spirit attached to it. In other words, they are worthless to someone who seeking a lost discarnate soul still attached to what is left of their mortal bodies.

Then we to go to a haunting tied to dark rituals that were conducted on or near the cemetery. The instruments and paraphernalia used are many times dumped on cemetery grounds as well.

You may ask yourself how we get a ghost from this. Many necromantic rituals from different belief systems use ghosts (lost souls) for divination, cursing or as messengers.

Sometimes these practitioners will bind a ghost to certain articles and then leave them in the cemetery so it will not follow them home. If you have heard of crossroads magic, it is something along the same line.

I myself have come across the remains of sacrificed animals and bags of ritual items that have been dumped inside cemetery grounds.

Inside graveyards, you might encounter non-human entities that have been summoned by someone who was dabbling with necromancy. Sometimes they know what they are doing, and other times they really do not, but are just lucky enough to conjure an entity and then leave it roaming around the cemetery.

Many of these practitioners also know how to lay down a barrier at the exit of the cemetery where these entities cannot leave. I have found them myself, especially in a small cemetery located in Brooksville, Florida.

Another entity that you can encounter when visiting cemetery grounds are called sentinels. They are summoned and bound to graveyards to make sure there is no desecration taking place. They are non-human. If seen at ground level they will appear as very tall shadows, but I have spotted then in trees as well, in the shape of some type of smaller animal. They are shadowy mostly watchers, and I believe they have the ability to shape shift.

You do not want to tangle with this type of entity. It is not a demon, but more along the lines of an elemental, but it is not that exactly either. Persons who have messed around in a cemetery, from knocking over tombstones to stealing bones could have one of them attach to them.

This is a very, very dark type of attachment, the haunting, and the repercussions for the human involved are severe, which can lead to death. There are not many people who are knowledgeable in how to deal with them. The ones that do will think twice before doing battle with it on your behalf. It can inflict deep psychological wounds on anyone trying to go against it.

This type of entity falls into the category that are very ancient and predate Judeo-Christian belief systems which is why it is so hard to break the hold they have on a human they have claimed. This is not a question of an exorcism; this is a question of breaking the connection and having it return to the graveyard where it originally came from.

Ancient and older cemeteries regardless of the culture or religious beliefs usually have more than one there. Newer ones do have them eventually, even though there is a tilting point when they start guarding the grounds.

They can be conjured and placed as sentinels by a human, but again this requires knowledge that is not commonly known.

My own theory is that they will start guarding burial grounds after a certain amount of dead are there, and this is very important, because it requires a certain amount of grieving to take place. I believe that this is why they stalk the grounds where humans come and mourn. They feed on sadness, despair and anger. You could argue that there is love, but when visiting a grave, unhappiness outweighs emotions that are more positive. Those that visit a cemetery usually go to mourn.

The good news is that these entities will ignore you if you do not do anything to desecrate the graves, or the dead in any way. If you happen to think you see one, I say, "think" because they are rarely seen and sometimes only as a tall shadows or the size of an animal perched in trees. Ignore it and walk away. Do not, let me emphasize the "do not" part, try to engage it, communicate with it or photograph it.

Now we come to the last type of haunting you will encounter in a cemetery. This is the same as a residual haunting found in a house. This is the accumulation of tears shed, heartbreak and despair expressed by humans on these grounds.

If you go periodically to visit a loved one, and leave within a little while, you should be OK, but if you spend a lot of time there, especially ghost hunting you can be influenced by the negative emotions that are contained in that environment. This is something to keep in mind when you are visiting graveyards.

I have heard of stories of gravediggers and cemetery caretakers, especially during the times where they lived on the grounds and worked there for many years, suffering from some type of negative influence.

ORBS

Do you know that saying about throwing out the baby with the bathwater? Well orbs falls into that category of paranormal anomaly that are disregarded, because in truth there are so many pictures out there that are just dust or bugs.

I will go on my own experience with orbs, which is that I have usually found them preceding some type of paranormal phenomena. They are seen afterward when reviewing film or photographs, as it is almost impossible to see them with the naked eye.

That is the value that I find in this type of anomaly, which is that its appearance is an announcement that some metaphysical event or being will be coming into that space; whether it is captured or not depends on different factors.

I do not examine orbs for faces or consider them actual spirits in a small ball form, and this is my own personal belief based on experience, and that I do set a high bar for accepting certain anomalies as authentic.

DOORWAYS BETWEEN DIMENSIONS

There are different theories as to what portals are, or if they actually exist at all.

Portals are described as doorways that can be opened or closed by rituals, and other times it is described as a rip between dimensions that stays open, letting through non-human entities, some with corporeal bodies others not, into our dimension.

These portals are said to be also doorways for human ghosts, and in some cases extraterrestrials.

I have had several conversations with different guests on my paranormal talk show *Stories of the Supernatural*, that claim these portals are used by UFOs and cryptids to disappear very quickly, which accounts why they cannot be found after a sighting.

Mirrors have frequently been linked to portals, and I have heard that those, which are placed on (inside of course) the outer walls of a home or structure, are the ones that can be used as such.

In my own personal experience as a paranormal investigator, I have found portals tied into digging into the earth.

I am referring to wells, basements and cellars. By this, I do not mean a shallow hole but something that usually needs some type of machinery to dig it out.

I have had two investigations where modern homes had a haunting that were centrally located in one of the corner rooms. It just so happened that both of these rooms were adjacent to water wells that were right next to the walls of these rooms.

I think this also accounts as to why subterranean areas of structures such as cellars and basements, always have such dark phenomena originating there. This also explains much of the strange activity tied to mines.

NATURE SPIRITS

Nature spirits also known as elementals are thought to be as old as the world. As their name implies they are believed to be tied to the elements, earth, fire, wind and water. They are non-human despite being paired with human-like beings such as fairies, leprechauns, gnomes, elves and others.

Like cemetery sentinels, they usually guard an area. Interaction with elementals was rare, but as urban areas expanded, humans found themselves inhabiting areas that are the domain of elementals.

Usually elementals have no interest in humans, and this is the best relationship to have with them. Indigenous cultures because of living closer to nature, understood this very clearly. They would appease it if necessary, but otherwise steered clear of them.

They do not operate with the same moral compass as humans. They do not see right or wrong the same way. They do not negotiate or make deals. Getting the attention of an elemental usually spells a problem for a human being. There are those that suggest there is an artificial form of elemental created by intense human thought, sometimes called a "tulpa", which eventually becomes independent from the control of its creator. I will cover this in more detail further on.

There are certain areas of land that have a history of negative experiences for humans who live on, or in some cases traverse it. Sometimes battles fought on the land, or massacres are thought of as the originating event that sets the stage for other human tragedies that take place there. However, the origin might be a conflict with some type of elemental spirit that predates any of those events.

Using the United States as reference, I am not referring to Native American burial grounds. Most indigenous people avoid these areas especially when it comes to disposing of their dead.

As an example, I will use a recent and well-known piece of land known as Skinwalker Ranch located in west Uintah County, Utah bordering the Ute Indian Reservation.

Linda Godfrey in her book *Monsters Among Us* described that the Utes avoided it at all costs. This fear was based on a Navajo legend, that for hundreds of years it was used by witches known as the yee naaldlooshii. The term translates loosely into "it travels fast on four feet".

These black magic practitioners were known for covering themselves only in coyote skins and traveling at night. They were said to practice cannibalism and necrophilia. One of their powers was the ability to transform into animal form, thus becoming skinwalkers.

Were the yee naaldlooshii elemental spirits? No, but the question should be why they would frequent this piece of land. It was no coincidence, and the answer lies in what was part of the land itself.

Sherman Ranch as it was originally known has had sightings of UFOs, werewolf-like creatures and other types of cryptids throughout the years.

There is a very strong possibility that there are very ancient elemental spirits in this area, as well as an interdimensional doorway. People and livestock that have lived on this land have not fared very well, and chances are they never will.

NOISY GHOSTS

These ghosts are better known as poltergeists. There is debate as to whether this phenomenon is only displaced psychokinetic (PK) energy from a teenager in the house, or a ghost who is using this energy to manifest their personality.

Poltergeists are some of the best-documented paranormal occurrences. There are reports that date back to ancient Roman times, and they are found in medieval accounts from different countries in Europe and China.

Many times, there are multiple witnesses. The thing about poltergeists is that activity usually stops as suddenly as it started. A common denominator is the presence of an adolescent, usually female in the household. These individuals are also dealing with some type of stressful situation in their lives. There is also a correlation with this being the target person that is harassed the most.

Poltergeists live up to their name, which translates into noisy ghosts. Phenomena are produced that is impossible to overlook. It could be lights switching on and off, items flying across the room, sounds of running steps, physically touching or hitting persons and interfering with electronics. These are just a few of the activities ascribed to poltergeists.

If you observe that this activity happens when a certain teenager is in the home, even sleeping in a room, or are they are in the room when things to start to happen, you might be dealing with a poltergeist.

Something very important to keep in mind is that the individual who is the agent is doing this on an unconscious level. Getting upset with a teenager in your household, or just telling them to "stop it!", is not going to work, usually it will only make it worse.

If the household is going through stressful times, then make a special effort to communicate with this person to see how they feel about what is going on. Notice I said ask how they feel, not what they think. You should do this without making them aware you are asking because you think they are the origin of the manifestation. Teenagers are weird so be ready to be rebuffed but put the offer out, when you least expect it they will take you up on the offer to talk about "it".

If there is no crisis going on in the home, then you might want to look closer at what is going on in this person's life that might be causing deep anxiety. Remembers, an individual's perception is their reality. If they confide in you do not pooh-pooh something that to you seems inconsequential, because obviously to them it is a cause of great emotional upset.

The following is a well-documented case that happened here in my hometown of Miami. It started December 1966 in the warehouse of a novelty wholesaler named Tropication Arts. The business owner Alvin Laubheim had two employees working in the 30' x 50' stocking area. The shipping clerks were an older man Curt Hagemeyer and a teenager named Julio Vasquez.

The business specialized in Florida-themed items so many of them were made of glass such as mugs and alligator ashtrays. It was no wonder that the owner became alarmed when during December several items broke when it appeared they had fallen off the shelves. He blamed it on the employees and on January 12, while showing them how to store the items, one of them flew off a shelf after he turned his back. Both Julio and Curt were fifteen feet away from the object. After this, the items started to frequently fall and fly off their place on shelves.

At other times, entire boxes would fall with a loud clatter from their secure perch on a shelf. The owner and the two employees spent the day picking up items, only to hear others fall in another part of the warehouse.

By January 23, items were crashing to the ground from the moment the business opened until it closed. Fifty-two incidents were noted on that day alone. One of the incidents involved a box full of glasses that weighed about fifteen pounds, and had moved twenty-four feet in order to fall upside down and smash all the glasses inside.

Police, delivery people even the business' insurance agent witnessed items moving or heard them crash out of sight.

Jack Roberts a reporter for the *Miami News* visited the business on the same day that Susy Smith, who wrote about psychic phenomena, was there as well. While he was talking to the owner, a box toppled off a shelf across the room. He saw that no one had been near it. He also saw a heavy light fixture sway overhead.

By November 1967, Susy Smith had issued her book *Prominent American Ghosts*. The incidents at Tropication Arts were included in it.

At one point, it was theorized that it was the spirit of a monkey that Alvin Laubheim had once owned. It had died a few months before the activity started. It was known for liking to break things and swing from the light fixtures.

Parapsychologist William Roll was alerted by Susy Smith about the incidents and he came to investigate. Initially nothing happened, then one day Dr. Roll observed a tense and angry Julio arguing with a female employee over an attempt his girlfriend's father was making to "exorcise" the ghost. She did not want to spoil the investigation with any type of "voodoo" at the business.

In his book *The Poltergeist*, Roll described the incident thus",I was looking at Julio, who was just about to reply to Miss Rambisz when the alligator ashtray crashed to the floor behind him... The cowbell remained in place, so the ashtray must have moved either over or around it. I could discover no way, in which Julio or anyone else could have produced this event normally. I had Julio and the others under observation and had examined the target area myself. No one had been near it since my last examination".

When Dr. Roll asked Julio how he felt he answered, "I feel happy, that things (the breakage) makes me feel happy; I do not know why".

A psychological test of Julio found evidence of anger, rebellion and aggressive impulses that he found unacceptable in himself. Julio's personal life confirmed that emotionally he was deeply distraught. In the months before the poltergeist activities, he had suffered frequent nightmares, some in which he was killed and saw himself at his own funeral. Ten days before the incidents started his stepmother had pressured him to leave the family house, which he did ten days before the incidents started.

Toward the end of January, there was a break-in at the business and he was a suspect. A few days later, he walked off with a ring from a jeweler's store that landed him in jail for six months. Once released Julio went through various jobs, and Dr. Roll reported that periodically he would get reports of objects still moving around him. By 1969, he was married, had a child and was working at a gas station. He was shot and seriously injured when he tried to stop gunmen who were trying to rob the business. Afterwards the connection with Julio was lost and no other information was provided as to what happened in his life.

This story gives you an idea of how unpredictable a poltergeist haunting can become. Even when all was said and done, Dr. Roll could never account as to why Julio's anger was transformed into PK energy.

The advice on handling poltergeist is to smudge as often as possible just to reduce the negativity that builds up from living in a house with this type of activity. You should try to reduce tension in the home. By this, I mean play happy music, watch comedy movies, go out to the park, anything that puts out positive energy and thoughts. It goes without saying that based on your religious or spiritual beliefs; you should incorporate this as well. Lastly, you will have to do this if not on a daily basis at the beginning at least on a weekly basis.

SHADOW PEOPLE

The shadow people that I am referring to are not human ghosts that are sometimes seen out of the corner of the eye or darting out of sight. These entities are described many times as being "darker than the darkness around them".

There are no recognizable features; some are described with red or yellow glowing eyes, others wearing some type of hat, or the outline of a monk's hood. There is debate as to whether they are human or not and I tend to put them in the non-human category. I have not had a firsthand encounter with one, but many people I have talked to describe the encounter as a negative experience.

Based on stories that have been related to me, a passage found in Dean Koontz's *Odd Thomas* series, comes the closest to a description of it, "Their infrequent appearance is always reason for alarm. These creatures seem to be spiritual vampires with knowledge of the future. They are drawn to places where violence or fiery catastrophe is destined to erupt, as if they feed on human suffering".

Most of the time, the impression is that they are male, broad shouldered, other times they appear as a swirling fog of black.

Shadow people are known to appear during periods of stress, unhappiness and even ill health being experienced by a person; and then they disappear. Some are known to attach to persons or families following them from house to house. They can disappear for months and years and then reappear when there is a crisis in the household. Others stay attached to a house, but I suspect their attachment is more to the land than the structure itself.

Another theory about shadow people is that they are a harbinger of death or catastrophe.

Shadow people are not always seen in a normal human form, as the following story describes concerning a nocturnal visit from one.

"I was just getting ready to go to sleep when I felt that I was not alone in the room. Nevertheless, I turned off the light and pulled the cover up to my chin. I was still awake when I heard heavy breathing coming from what I realized in some alarm was the top of my bookshelf. There was some illumination coming in from a streetlight outside the window, and I looked at the three-foot space between the ceiling and the top of the bookshelf. There I saw an area that was darker than the surroundings. This compact shadow was where the breathing was coming from. I felt that it was watching me in a malevolent way.

I turned the lights on, and even though I could not see it anymore, I knew it was still there. I could hear it breathing. My sister was across the room asleep. She was none the wiser to what was happening.

I was sitting on the edge of my bed when I heard it jump down to the floor. I heard a slight shuffling as it approached me, all the while I was still hearing the breathing sound. Then I felt the temperature drop. The cold spot was only three feet tall. I lost my nerve, turned off the light and got back in bed with the covers drawn up. I heard it reach the edge of my bed, and the cold was more intense.

It stayed next to my bed for a bit and then jumped into it. I felt that it was trying to get into my mind, and the more I resisted the angrier it got. I then felt it crawl on top of my chest. I could feel its weight and the cold that came with it. I felt its hands around my throat, and I turned my face so that it would not be able to press its face to mine. It could not squeeze that hard.

Its legs were short, and it had big feet. It appeared it did not have knees like a human. I only felt three fingers around my neck and they felt longer than normal. All I kept thinking was that I was not going to let it into my head. I fell asleep, and I never felt its presence again. I am glad I did not turn on the lights and see what it looked like.

Eventually I got married and had a daughter. One day when she was six years old, she came into our bedroom. All she kept saying was that she had woken up and seen a little man looking at her over the edge of her bed. This was the only description she would give that he looked evil. She refused to go back to her room for over a month, and until this day, she has not forgotten what she saw. I had never said anything about what I had experienced. So far, neither my family members nor I have had another experience with this creature".

Shadow people are one of those phenomena that you must consistently address once you are aware of their presence. Items that it would be good to have around at all times are sweet grass and desert sage. This would be in addition to smudging and the use of any spiritual or religious practice you want to use. If you have heavy drapes, I would urge you to change them to something filmy or draw them away from the window. In other words, increase the lighting in your space either with daylight or artificially. Dispel the man-made shadows as much as you can.

Like any other type of negative influence from an entity, one of the most important things to guard against is isolation.

I suggest these tactics, for one of two reasons. The first is that you are taking charge of the situation, which is very important. Secondly, if this is a human entity, this approach will be very effective. Human ghosts that are seen as shadows are sometimes unable to have enough energy to materialize fully. They are normal height as a regular person, and even though they might be scary for a moment, you do not feel any malevolence. They make an effort not to be seen. The thing is, that when it concerns shadow people, these are the minority.

If after thirty days you do not see any positive results, by this I mean not that it is resolved totally, but being just as bad or worse, then start looking for a paranormal team to help you.

Many people will argue that shadow people or hat man is a recent paranormal phenomenon and that they are just part of a trend.

Not so, I just think that with the advances of the internet and the ability to share information it is just easier for people to retell of their experiences.

This was a story told to me in the 1980s by a friend I used to work with. We were talking about ghosts, and she told me about an experience she had as a teenager. One night she woke up in the middle of the night and saw a tall man with a top hat standing at the foot of her bed, staring malevolently at her. She lived in a modern, two-bedroom apartment with her parents in a suburb of Miami. She hid under the covers, filled with dread. She knew this was not a real human being, and she could never account as to why she would be seeing this in her room. Within a year, her mother passed away from an existing heart condition.

DEMONIC ENTITIES

The following entities I will be describing are considered non-human. They have never been human. Their only aim when it comes to the living is to cause harm; physical and psychological. Handling these types of entities is not a DIY project. You need to call in paranormal investigators who are experienced in handling this type of phenomena. The good news is that this is not as common as it is made out to be in the media and in paranormal shows.

One of the clues that you might be dealing with a demonic entity is that they are accompanied by a foul odor. Not all the times, but I know of cases where people have even torn up floorboards looking for what they think is a dead animal causing the bad odor. The smell will disappear just as suddenly as it appeared. There are times when the living will hear an animal-like growl coming out of thin air or out of a darkened room or a corner.

Aside from poltergeists, the ability to move and throw heavy objects is a hallmark of a demonic entity. Over the years, I have spoken to several investigators who find a correlation between violent manifestations and demonic entities being at the root of it.

The goal is to cause fear and upheaval for the humans living in a place. What is more frightening than to have items thrown violently across the room, or have a lamp swing hard from side to side above your head? This is part of their psychological and emotional attack. Once they instill fear in you, they can terrify you in a multitude of ways.

There have been reports of scratches and bite marks to persons they have targeted. This can be accompanied by a heavy feeling in the room, and dramatic changes in temperature, usually right before a manifestation of some type.

They invade your mind by giving you horrible nightmares, making you fear falling asleep. If want to undermine a person's sanity, try withholding sleep from them.

What they want is to control you, or someone in the household so that they can be easily manipulated. It strives to bring out the worse emotions and thoughts a human can experience.

There are times when only a specific person is affected and phenomena will only happen when they are alone. This is an effort to divide and conquer. A person can feel very isolated if they believe there is some degree of disbelief coming from anyone else in the home. What of course follows is that human beings will act out negatively when they find themselves in this type of situation.

Persons who suffer from mental illness are many times targeted. If a person is going through an emotional crisis or depression, this vulnerability will attract demonic attention. Families that are dysfunctional, or where there is a constant state of upheaval will also get their unwanted attention. Why? Because distressed persons are easy to manipulate and they feed off the fear, anger and sadness generated by the living.

It is during this process that negative thoughts can be put in a person's mind. Unfortunately, they sometimes act out in ways that are unlike them, either physically or verbally. During this process, a person does have free will, but fear is used as a crowbar to divorce a person from their common sense.

Depending on the emotional makeup of the person that is being targeted, a demonic entity will disguise itself as a child. I discussed this earlier and what are the dangers when letting down your guard.

There are instances of demons disguising themselves with the appearance of a loved one that has died.

Some paranormal researchers believe that demons can attach to a person or to a family and follow them from place to place.

I want to stress that this type of haunting is rare, but if you suspect this is what is happening, then do not waste time and reach out for help as soon as you can find a qualified group or individual to work with. In the meantime, do not do confrontations, but do continue to bring light into your household. This has the effect of scraping your nails on the chalkboard to a demon. This type of resistance, when consistent is very effective and not giving this entity your fear or anger is smart warfare.

Be prepared that when you do reach out to someone for help, activity will die down. It will do this to lull you into complacency that everything is better. Do not be fooled!

SEXUAL ATTACKS

Entities that attack humans sexually are demonic. Each is different depending on which sex they are targeting. An incubus is male, a succubus is female. Stories regarding attacks by incubi or succubi go back for centuries. An attack by one of these demons is seldom a one-time event. They return slowly deteriorating a person's health, their mental state and in some cases resulting in their death.

A well-publicized case was that of the Smurl family which had this type of disturbing aspect to it.

In 1973, the family had moved into a duplex built in 1896. Jack and Janet Smurl were both practicing Catholics, and they lived on one side of the duplex and Jack's parents lived in the other.

For the first year and a half nothing happened, but that all changed when several appliances and parts of the house appeared to be damaged by claws. In 1975, their oldest daughter said she saw people floating around in her room.

It did not take long before the Smurl family realized the entire structure was haunted as more and more phenomena happened. Footsteps were heard on the stairs, strange unpleasant smells wafted through the house, and rocking chairs moved when they were empty.

By 1977, the Smurls had four children, and it was not until 1985 that the experiences became truly sinister. The entity started to mimic human voices and use obscene language. The family was physically attacked, including their pet German shepherd. Different animal noises were heard throughout the house, including pig-like snorting coming from behind the walls.

The noises were so loud that neighbors would hear screams when the Smurls were not at home.

In 1986, the Smurls contacted Ed and Lorraine Warren. The demonologists used different methods, but only prayer and holy water seemed to quiet it down.

At one point Jack Smurl was raped by a scaly-skinned succubus. It had the face of a hag and the body of a young woman. Janet suffered her own rape at the hands of an incubus. One of their own daughters was nearly raped by the incubus as well.

An exorcism was conducted at the house by a priest brought in by the Warrens, but the haunting continued. A second exorcism was done by the same priest, but nothing changed. The demon even accompanied the family when they went on a camping trip to the Poconos.

The Smurls were warned that the demon would follow them if they moved, and after repeated refusals from the Catholic Church in Pennsylvania, they publicized their plight to the local media. They kept their identity anonymous, but the demon increased its attacks because of their appearance. Jack saw it as a two-legged pig, and he was raped once again by the succubus.

In 1986, they published their story in the newspaper, this time there was no anonymity, and their property was overrun by the media and onlookers. Perhaps forced by the publicity, on August 22, *The Lakeland Ledger* reported the Catholic Church was taking the reports seriously, "but are unconvinced it is the work of a demon".

The Smurls brought in a medium named Mary Alice Rinkman. She claimed there were four entities. One was an old woman named Abigail, another was an unidentified human entity. There was a man named Patrick who had killed his unfaithful wife and her lover; he had then been lynched by a mob. The last was the dark demon that had terrorized the family the most.

In 1988, the family moved from the home, and whether it was the change of location or the prayers and blessings done, the Smurls claimed they were free of the haunting.

Sexual attacks are usually part of a larger array of paranormal phenomena, as demonstrated by what happened with the Smurl family.

Seeking help with this type of encounter is a must, however there are things that you can do between visits from a paranormal team or someone in the clergy. Remember you have to live in this space when those helping you leave and go back to their home.

All the prior instructions given should be incorporated into a "daily" ritual for you and your family. If there is any physical or emotional trauma in your background, especially in childhood you should seek out medical help and therapy.

THE NIGHT HAG

Night Hag is also known as Old Hag Syndrome and in layman's terms, sleep paralysis. Persons describe coming wide-awake and unable to move. They feel a pressure on their chest, and have trouble drawing in a breath. It is accompanied by a feeling of fear and dread. Persons have described not only feeling the pressure on their upper body, but strange smells, approaching footsteps and in some cases a visual of what the entity is. Some only see glowing eyes, or what is described as an old, haggard woman. The spell is broken when they can move or actually utter a sound out of their mouth.

Both men and women of different ages claim having this type of irrational experience. It is different for each person; however, one common theme is the feeling of intense fear. Over one-fifth of the United States population has described this type of encounter, usually when they have fallen asleep on their back. Sometimes it lasts for months, other times for years.

The medical field calls it sleep paralysis, and it is explained as what happens in the transition state between REM sleep and waking up. During REM sleep, body movements are turned off, and when we awake, they return. Sometimes these two functions are out of sync, creating the "frozen" feeling described that can seem to last an eternity even though it is only a few seconds. Hypnagogic and hypnopompic experiences produce the hallucinations; however, there is no explanation as to "why" this happens, and to some people and not others.

TULPAS

This word was introduced into our lexicon by Alexandra David-Néel (1868-1969) who was a Belgian-French explorer and spiritualist who traveled extensively into Tibet, a country that little was known about at the turn of the 20th century. She snuck into Lhasa disguised as a man, and took only an exploration partner named Lama Aphur Yongden with her since foreigners were prohibited from visiting. She wrote thirty books throughout her life.

As a young woman she studied Theosophical teachings and joined several secret societies, including reaching the 30th degree in the mixed Scottish Rite of Freemasonry. By the time she was 21 years old she had become a Buddhist.

In 1929, she published *Magic and Mysticism in Tibet* where she described her encounter with a Tibetan phenomenon, which translated from the local dialect into the word tulpa.

She described it as an illusion created by a spiritual entity or a person who can concentrate sufficiently to give their thought form animus.

They can be anything, and once well-developed can be mistaken for real. If the tulpa is formed as a human, it can eventually become independent of their creator and even outlive them.

The Tibetan monks claimed that spirits and deities used tulpas to create manifestations or to interact with the living. Usually it was monks who were well-versed in creating one, but a regular person could do it if they focused on a thought too much.

In the book *The Secret Lives of Alexandra David-Neel* (2002), there is a description of when David-Neel decided to create her own tulpa. She envisioned it as a short, fat, jolly monk. This process took a few months, including visualizing details about this entity she wanted to create, and seeing it doing things around her.

She then ended the "creation process", and continued in her travels. She started to see the monk doing activities expected of a traveler in the group. Even though she was no longer concentrating on him, she started to feel him brush past her and once she thought she felt his hand on her shoulder.

Once it was independent, she realized that it was changing. It was no longer fat and jolly, but changed to being more slender-looking and had a malicious look in its eyes. There was no doubt that she was losing control of her tulpa. Once David-Neel received reports that others coming to her camp had seen him she decided to dissolve it, which took six months to accomplish.

Another word for tulpa is a thought form. In paranormal circles there is a belief that repetitive, negative thoughts from a living person can create an entity that will haunt a person, and by extension the people living with this person.

In recent years, you will find instructions on the Internet on how to create a tulpa, which I consider is extremely dangerous, especially by someone who has a weak grip on reality. There have been reports of people claiming that the tulpa they created has told them to harm themselves.

You need not look further than the experiment described by David-Neel who was an experienced mystic, when she realized the entity she had created needed to be terminated.

ALEXANDRA DAVID NEELS (1868-1969)
AN INTREPID EXPLORER & MYSTIC SHE SNUCK INTO
THE FORBIDDEN CITY OF LHASA DISGUISED AS A MAN

THE MESSENGERS

Encounters with angels have been reported from time immemorial until present-day. Their role has many times been ascribed as messengers from God or intermediaries between human beings and the Divine. Their visitation is connected with comfort, and in some cases as guardians.

Even though these entities are non-human, they are mostly seen in human form. Just like Marian apparitions, they are mostly preceded by ancient, sweet scents such as sandalwood, rose and frankincense. They have also been described as brilliant white light in a roughly human figure. They have been seen both with and without wings. They are known to come and deliver messages in dreamtime, or just a message heard in the person's ear.

Angels have also been embodied in the guise of a kind or protective stranger. They might appear out of nowhere when a person is in need of help right away, and just as mysteriously disappear. The persons involved always take them as another human being.

Contrary to some beliefs that guardian angels could be deceased loved ones, guardian angels assigned at a person's birth are strictly angelic beings. Just because you have a guardian angel with you at all times, does not preclude asking other angels to help or intercede on your behalf.

I will tell you my own story about what I think looking back, was not one but two angelic beings that came to my rescue.

This was during the 1980s. My children were small and my husband had agreed to babysit for me while I visited with a high school friend I had not seen in years.

It was a weekday, and after eating dinner, we talked for hours, catching up on stories and gossip. I lived literally 30 miles away at the other end of the county, and by the time I started back, it was late, close to midnight.

On my way to get on a main highway, I went through an industrial area that was really deserted. Remember this was a weekday and late at night. All of a sudden, I heard the sickening thumping of when your car has a flat tire. I pulled off the road, and inspected my tire that was very flat. I had a spare in my trunk, but I had no idea on how to change it.

There were no gas stations, and again this was the time before everyone had a cellular phone and the popularity of roadside service. I faced a real dilemma about getting back home, but make no mistake I was worried for my safety.

First, I had to try to find a phone, and then call my husband who would have to come across the county with three small children who were already sleeping.

Just as I was looking at my car to make sure it was really off the road, two young men approached me. When I say they came out of nowhere, I literally mean that. I had been scanning the street and sidewalk on either side of me just in case someone suspicious was coming towards me and I had seen no one.

Their appearance was so sudden that I did not have a chance to jump in my car. They were in their twenties, and they asked me very politely if I needed help with my tire. I said yes, and made sure to keep my distance, even though I felt no sense of menace coming from them.

I opened the trunk and between both of them, they changed it within ten minutes. I offered them some money, but they declined and just walked off. I jumped in my car because I had to get to a phone and let my husband know I was okay, and that I was headed home. As I drove up the street in the direction they had walked off in, there was no one there.

The closest housing was some rundown apartments that were at least half a mile away. There is no way they could have gone anywhere near that distance in the space of two or three minutes. The only buildings around there were factories that were closed, and the empty parking lots around them. That is my angel story. Whether they were really angels or not, what they did for me was angelic.

GUARDIAN SPIRITS

Personal protective spirits are also thought to join a person at birth. Just like the guardian angel, its mission is to look out for the person it is assigned to. Even though one has free will, it tries to steer its possessor out of trouble through precognition or clairvoyance. In some belief systems, one acquires a guardian spirit through a vision quest, usually at the time of puberty.

CHAPTER 4
WHY ARE THEY HAUNTING

When you determine why a ghost is haunting a certain place you are well on your way to moving it on. Sometimes the identity and reason will never become known and other times it is obvious.

I do want to caution you that sometimes the usual suspect is not the actual origin of the haunting. For example, if you find out someone died in the home, committed suicide or had a funeral wake in the home that is not an automatic haunter. Only less than a hundred years ago it was commonplace for people to be born and die at home. It was also common to have wakes in the home, and then from there the family and those attending would make their way to a church or similar place for a religious ceremony and then to the cemetery.

With our modern day sensibilities, where people die in nursing homes or hospitals, we forget that was not always the case. Which by the way, with the high cost of going to the hospital for treatment versus an emergency or a trauma situation, more people are opting for natural births, and to die at home if they have a terminal illness or if they are very elderly.

OWNERSHIP

This type of ghost is very common. If they built the home, if they lived there a very long time or if towards the end of their life they were a recluse, this could contribute as to why a human stays stuck in the place they used to live in.

If they are confused as to the fact that they are dead, they will do what most humans do, which is to gravitate to what is familiar to you. When they see that their belongings are gone and there are strangers inhabiting the place that was once theirs, they can make an effort to drive out the living.

When homeowners complain about being watched by a malevolent spirit, it might just be a prior homeowner giving them a dirty look.

If you know who the prior owner was, you can address them by name and tell them that they are dead, and that they do not need a house anymore. If you do not know who the prior owner was, it is worth the effort to research it. However, do not romanticize the history of any of the people that lived there, especially if they had tragic lives or deaths. The ultimate aim is to help them move on and for you to have true ownership of the place you live in.

There are going to be cases where you just do not know who is haunting a certain location, but sometimes these discarnates are just waiting for someone to acknowledge who they were, or expose the truth of what happened to them.

The Ghosts of Chillingham Castle

The following is a story of a ghost that was known to haunt an ancient place in England known as Chillingham Castle. It is located in Northumberland, close to the Scottish border. The original structure dates back to the 12th century when it was a monastery. Due to its location, it became a command post for the English army when it battled the Scots, and in turn, it was besieged several times by the Scottish army.

There was a room known as the "Pink Room". This was where the phantom of the "Radiant Boy" or the "Blue Boy" was said to appear only at certain times. It was said that when the clock tower sounded the stroke of midnight, cries and moans would be heard, as if a child was in agony. His identity has never been established; even though some surmise it was a young lord of Tankerville who died an accidental and very tragic death.

In December 29, 1822, *The Examiner* described an incident where Lord Londonderry encountered the ghost of the "radiant boy" -

> "He retired to bed but his candles had not been long extinguished, when he perceived a light gleaming on the draperies of the lofty canopy over his head. Conscious that there was no fire in the grate, that the curtains were closed, that the chamber had been in perfect darkness but a few moments before, he supposed that some intruder must have accidentally entered his apartment; and turning hastily round to the side from which the light proceeded, saw to his infinite astonishment, not the form of any human visitor, but the figure of a fair boy, who seemed to be garmented in rays of mild and tempered glory, which beamed palely from his slender form like the faint light of the declining moon, and rendered the objects which were nearest to him dimly and indistinctly visible. The spirit stood at some short distance from the side of the bed. Certain that his own faculties were not deceiving him but suspecting that he might be imposed upon by the ingenuity of some of the numerous guests who were then visiting in the same house, Lord Londonderry

proceeded towards the figure. It retreated before him. As he slowly advanced, the form, with equal paces, slowly retired. It entered the vast arch of the capacious chimney, and then sunk into the earth. Lord L. returned to his bed, but not to rest."

In 1929, Lady Tankerville gave the following account of this little ghost that haunted her home, Chillingham Castle:

"Always the noises came from a spot nearest to a passage cut through the ten-foot thick wall into the adjoining tower. It was in the adjoining tower that the bones of a boy of tender years and some fragments of a blue dress were later discovered. These poor remains were reverently removed and decently interred in consecrated ground".

After the burial, the haunting stopped, or so it was assumed, as the castle was abandoned in 1932 due to the high cost of its upkeep. The contents were sold, the gardens became overgrown and the roofs fell in. It was not until fifty years later when it was bought and renovated by Sir Humphry Wakefield.

Without knowing the specifics, chances are that this child died tragically and through circumstances that demanded a secret burial where his body was immured. Once his remains were discovered, it appears he was released from reliving the events that ended in his death.

LEONORA, COUNTESS OF TANKERVILLE
SHE LIVED AT CHILLINGHAM CASTLE +
HAD SEVERAL GHOSTLY EXPERIENCES
c. MID-1920s

CHILLINGHAM CASTLE (ABOVE) + THE BEDROOM WHERE THE
RADIANT BOY WAS SEEN C.1929

THE SPIRIT OF THE LAND

Many families can never account as to why their house is haunted. I myself have been called to properties built in a new development that had paranormal events from the moment the family moved in.

In one case, the new home was surrounded by undeveloped lots that were still under construction. I happened to have arrived towards the end of the workday. We had already determined that everything started as soon as the family moved to this new house. I decided to take a gamble and speak to a couple of men who were working across the street. Most of the construction activity had ended for the day.

I came quickly to the point and asked if they had experienced anything weird when they were working in any of the houses. If it were not for the fact that they would have weirded out and ended the conversation at that moment, I would have taken a picture of their faces. The look they traded spoke volumes.

They both said that they had experienced seeing shadows, or hearing crunching of footsteps outside where they were working and nobody would show up. They said this was especially witnessed early in the morning, or toward the end of the day. In some houses, not all of them, tools would be misplaced and found in weird places, if at all. Obviously, this was when there was less noise and movement coming from construction taking place.

They told me about an older man who was the security guard during the night, who often reported seeing shadow people running from yard to yard. The security guard had confided in them that he had stopped going into the half-built structures when one time he had been walking on the first floor of a house that only had the walls erected. There were no windows, and just the roof trusses, when he heard growling coming from the second floor of the structure. A chill air enveloped him and he ran back to his car. Despite his sightings of shadow people, none of the building materials or appliances that were pre-installed prior to closing was ever stolen.

They ducked out saying that they had to leave, and I could tell I was lucky to have gotten the information from them that I had.

The point is that despite moving into a new development out in the suburbs, there is no guarantee that other structures were not there before. The following is a true story that could be applied to any piece of land across the United States and produce a haunting that no one can account for.

This is a story about a house near the Conesville Mines in Ohio. The incident described happened after the Civil War.

A family had moved to the area in 1898. They went to see a house that was for rent. They met the owner at the property, and the father noted that a well curb has been shoved off its base, and lay on the ground nearby. This left the well exposed and the father asked the owner about this. The owner got nervous but explained it by saying that some mischievous neighbor boys had pushed it off. With its windlass and roof it was very heavy, and it took four men to lift it back into place.

The family went ahead and rented the property and as they were moving in, they saw that the well-curb was off its base again. When the father contacted the owner about it, he said it had probably blown over in a windstorm. The father was doubtful since there had not been any inclement weather, but since he had just gotten a job in the nearby mines he decided to stay.

A few days later while he was at work, when the local men found out where he lived, they asked him, "Has the old lady kicked off the well-curb yet?"

They told him that one of the prior owners, an old lady had drowned herself in the well, and that her ghost came back to push the housing from its base. A few days later, the family found the well-curb once again off its base. The father moved the family out.

Chances are that the piece of land where this house and the well were located on has long since been demolished, and there are none to remember what the history of the haunted well was. If a house was ever built on it, maybe they heard thumping coming up from the floor, or even the apparition of an old woman.

WELL WITH A WIND LASS + ROOF

The Forgotten Ones

The following is another story that was well publicized due to a book that was written about it in 1991.

It was the early 1980s and Ben and Jean Williams moved to a new development in Crosby, Texas a suburb of Houston.

They were one of the first families to move there, and they noticed something unusual in their yard, which was an oak tree with a carving on it. It was an arrow with two lines under it. Like most people would have done, they dismissed it.

Another family who had moved early on into the neighborhood was the Haneys. They decided to build a pool, but barely had the contractors started their work when an older, black man named Jasper Norton came to their home with a warning. He told them they were about to dig up two graves. He knew where they were because he had dug them. In fact, he had dug 20 of at least 60 pauper graves. The last burial had been in 1939.

The work continued, and sure enough, two old pine boxes were discovered. They contacted the local sheriff and with the help of the coroner, they were officially exhumed. Two wedding rings found in the graves identified them as Charles and Betty Thomas, slaves that had been freed after the Civil War.

Further investigation found that this piece of land was actually the Black Hope Cemetery. It had been part of the McKinney Plantation owned by the Mercer McKinney family. Freed slaves had worked there and this piece of land had been given to them in order to bury their dead. An entire black community was built on this section of the land with schools, churches, a cemetery, until a fire demolished it

The cemetery had never been officially recognized by Harris County. The carved oak in the Williams' property was actually a grave marker.

The Haneys tried to find Thomas family members who could reclaim the bodies but none could be located. They decided to reinter them on their property, which kicked off a series of paranormal events in all the homes that sat on the graveyard.

Some of the phenomena reported were electronics and faucets turning on and off by themselves. Any gardens they would plant would die out despite their best attention towards it.

Judith Haney once heard the sliding glass door downstairs open, and she believed it was her husband returning home from his late shift at work. She called out to him, and receiving no answer, she went downstairs to find the door securely locked and her husband had not returned yet. The following day she could not find her shoes, but then found them outside sitting on top of Betty Thomas' grave.

The Williams family had coffin-shaped sinkholes appear in their yard, that no amount of filling in could make disappear. Shadow people, distant conversations and bad smells pervaded their house.

Both the Haneys and the Williams felt they had been deceived when they bought the properties. The Haneys were unsuccessful in suing the housing company and ended up declaring bankruptcy and moving away.

The Williams sued the developer but were faced with a conundrum, which was they had to prove the land was a forgotten graveyard, however state law prohibited them from excavating.

Seeing no other option then to prove their case the Williams decided to dig. Jean Williams was digging and unexpectedly started to feel very tired. Her 30-year-old daughter Tina took over and 30 minutes later Tina collapsed after complaining of chest pains. She was rushed to the hospital, but by the time she arrived there, she was brain dead. Three days later the family removed her from life support. She had suffered a heart attack.

The heartbroken Williams family returned the house to the lender and moved to Montana. By then the original eight houses built had been abandoned by the families who had bought them. In 1991, they published a book about their experiences, titled *The Black Hope Horror, The True Story of a Haunting*.

In a 2007 *Chron* article, it was reported that Tom Hunt had moved into the house that belonged to the Haneys, and claimed that though it was strange to have two graves in his yard, nothing paranormal had happened to them.

Kayla Lengacher who occupied the home where the Williams had lived, claimed the same thing, except for one incident. She described where she heard what sounded like a cougar screaming above her window, and when she went to investigate could not find anything.

Another neighbor also echoed the same experience of nothing significant being experienced, but there were a few stories that leave no doubt that the occupants of the Black Hope graveyard still haunt the area.

One complained of slamming doors, which he attributed to drafts however, his mother will not stay there after dark. Perhaps it is because she has seen black orbs floating in one of the rooms of the house. Another time she went to the restroom in the house and she heard a man's voice breathing very heavy close to her. Soon after that, her 3-year-old granddaughter told her "I saw that brown man and he tried to pick me up". She was perplexed how this small child could know that the houses were built on an African American graveyard.

Even until this day the identity of all those buried there remains a mystery. Sources say there is a higher than average turnover in homes that were built in Section 8 of the subdivision – The Black Hope section

This story illustrates that land developers themselves can be ignorant of what used to be on a piece of land they purchased.

The advice is to sage down a new home, and salt the property line even if it is sold to you as a brand new home.

This should be done before you bring in any of your belongings or furniture.

I have handled cases where paranormal phenomena were strictly in the original portion of a structure, and nothing ever happened in a new addition that was later constructed. The point being, that even if you mostly demolish an older structure and build a new one on the foundation you should metaphysically cleanse the finished product, or even better, do it before you start the construction.

GHOSTLY PASSAGEWAYS

There is a belief that ghosts use wells as passageways into the physical realm. If a house is built on top of it, or left in place in the cellar of a structure it could precipitate ghostly manifestations. Covering the opening will only make it worse.

It appears that an opening into the earth as well as the presence of water is the perfect conduit for entities.

Bodies of water, whether they are lakes, inlets, rivers or streams have always been tied to elemental spirits or undines. Humans would leave offerings on the shore, and in some cases, the dead were deposited there as well, in the belief that this was the entry point into the afterlife. There is another belief that ghosts and supernatural beings cannot cross running water.

The same power that does not allow evil entities to cross water is used in purification rites and for divination. That is the reason why healing springs have shrines and churches built in their proximity.

IT IS ALL IN YOUR HEAD

Psychological problems by people living in a place can create or worsen ghostly manifestations. This also explains why some persons experience a haunting and others are impervious to the phenomena.

The following case was investigated by Nandor Fodor in the 1930s. It took place in England and was detailed in his book *The Haunted Mind*.

In June 1934, the Keel family (a pseudonym) moved to Ash Manor House that had original structures that dated back to the 13th century.

They were in ignorance that the property had a reputation for being haunted even though two previous owners who had lived there, each for several years, had not complained about any haunting. One has to wonder though what Mrs. Keel thought when the prior owner mentioned that all the servants had run away.

The first persons to experience any phenomena was the Keel's 16-year-old daughter and the servants who heard the sounds of someone walking around in the attic.

Five months after they had moved in Mr. Keel was awakened by three heavy bangs on his bedroom door. He went to his wife's room who had also heard the noise, but there was no one in the hallway. The following two nights the banging on the bedroom doors continued.

A week later, he left to go out of town, and during that time nothing happened, however the day he returned, he was filled with foreboding. So much so that he tried not to fall asleep, but he was overcome and suddenly came awake when he heard one single bang on the bedroom door.

Standing in the doorway, he described, "a little, oldish man, dressed in a green smock, very muddy breeches and gaiters, a slouch hat on his head and a handkerchief around his neck".

Thinking that his culprit was a servant, he jumped up to grab him by the shoulder, and he fainted when his hand went through the apparition.

His wife was astonished when he came to her room babbling about what happened to him. She left to find some brandy to give her husband, when she saw the little old man still standing in the doorway of her husband's room.

She described his eyes as "malevolent and horrid" and his mouth dribbled with saliva. Making the same mistake as her husband, she thought he was a vagrant who had broken into the house. When she tried to strike him, her hand went through him. She ran off with the brandy in hand.

He was dubbed the green man. He was usually seen by Mr. Keel, as his favorite spot to appear at was in front of the chimney in Mr. Keel's room. This was also the area where there was a priest's hole.

Mrs. Keel once observed that he had a wound on his neck, which indicated that his throat had been cut, and she suspected that he had been immured behind the chimney wall.

All the servants quit, and the Keels sought help from outside sources. Individuals who claimed expertise in the field failed, and things got worse after an exorcism conducted by a priest. Two lay exorcists claimed that the house had been built on a Druidic circle, which is why the formal exorcism by the priest had worsened the situation.

They said that ghost was named Henry Knowles and that in 1819 he committed suicide by slitting his own throat after a milkmaid rejected his advances.

In 1936, two years after they had moved there the Keels connected with Fodor. He spent time in the house, including the haunted bedroom but did not experience any phenomena.

He returned the following month with psychic Eileen Garrett. Her impression was of a different ghost, she described a fair-haired man who had been a prisoner and who had been involved in some type of failed rebellion. He had been tortured and left crippled in order to extract information from him. The papers he carried where hidden in the chimney.

Garrett who was a psychic medium, allowed her control named Uvani to speak through her and explain why the ghost had manifested. He said that when an atmosphere of unhappiness is created by the living, a spirit with a similar feeling would draw upon it to relive their suffering. Uvani explained that during the 15th century, a prison had existed nearby where persons had died in misery. Many of them lingered about, and were immediately attracted to the living that mirrored the energy they had died with.

The entity then possessed Garrett directly and gave his name as Charles Edward Huntingdon. He complained that his land had been robbed by the Earl of Huntington. He had been separated from his family and left to rot in jail. What he wanted more than anything was vengeance. They told the ghost of his true state and that he needed to move on, and join his family on the other side. He agreed reluctantly.

The intervention by Eileen Garrett with the noble Charles Edward, did not resolve the drooling "green man" because within twenty-four hours he was seen again by Mr. Keel. He described where the ghost was trying to speak despite having an exposed windpipe from a slash at his throat.

Contrary to being agitated at the return of the ghost, Mr. Keel appeared smug that Fodor was unable to banish it.

Fodor brought Garret back for another session, but this time the Keels were not present. Garrett's control Uvani said that the Keels were using the unhappy soul in order to embarrass each other, which is why neither wanted the ghost to move on.

When Fodor confronted Mrs. Keel with the last message imparted by Uvani, she confessed that her husband was a secret homosexual and a great deal of tension existed between them. She was taking drugs in order to deal with the situation, and her daughter resented her obsession with her husband, despite the fact that he did not even want to share a bedroom with her. The ghost diverted attention from a problem that lay unresolved between them.

Mr. Keel agreed that what Uvani had described was true, but now he felt that he was being possessed by the entity. However Keel's admission about Uvani's description of what was anchoring the ghost there, achieved what the exorcism had failed to do. The spirit was not seen again.

They investigated historical records to find any proof that Charles Edward had existed but were unable to find any. They knew there was less chance of any record existing for Henry Knowles who was probably a servant or tradesman.

This story again confirms a point I will return to repeatedly regarding the mental state of those living in a house where paranormal phenomena is being experienced. It is a very simple theory of like attracting like.

NO NEED TO RSVP

Inviting a ghost into your home is much easier than most people believe. The most obvious is participating in a séance or using a Ouija board without knowing how to open and close the session. At first glance these might appear to be just scary games and harmless.

What happens when you try to communicate with ghosts is that you open a portal that connects two dimensions. Chances are that a negative entity will immediately recognize the ignorant novice and take advantage of the opportunity

This holds true even when trying to communicate with an entity that is already in your home. If there is one unwritten rule in the metaphysical world, it is the power of the invitation.

Another way is through dabbling in the occult without understanding exactly what metaphysical doors you are trying to open. There has always been interest in the occult, but it was usually an underground pursuit. There were different approaches to this secret knowledge such as Theosophy, Rosicrucianism, witchcraft, Satanism, necromancy and black magic among others.

When you have a dark spirit at the other end of the line, the invitation they seek translates into getting you to freely give them permission to interact with you. They are savants when it comes to knowing a person's vulnerabilities, and they play upon these weaknesses to gain trust; if deception is necessary, then so be it, it is just a means to an end.

One of the best true-life descriptions was detailed by Edwin Becker in his riveting books, *True Haunting 1 & 2*. I have interviewed Ed Becker on *Stories of the Supernatural*, and even forty years after these events, he is still very insistent about staying clear of dabbling in the occult.

In *True Haunting 2*, he takes up the story where a televised exorcism in his home had failed. A psychic who had tried to help the family, Joseph DeLouise, had tried cleansing the home, but he had not been successful.

They had tenants renting the downstairs flat. Not until many years later did they become aware how deeply affected they were by the dark spirits that had failed to be ousted from the building. His tenant asked to break the lease, and when Ed was finally able to speak to the husband many years later, he was told that this man considered that the home had ruined his marriage. Shortly after they had moved out, his wife left with his child and he lost track of them for thirty-five years.

Ed's sister April moved into the empty apartment. As much as Ed and his wife were repelled by the paranormal phenomena they had endured, his sister was fascinated and started using a Ouija board. Ed's wife Marsha who was at home during the day was the first one that noticed her sister-in-law's personality changes.

April was described by Marsha Becker as a happy wife and mother. Slowly her personality and habits started to change for the worse. Joseph DeLouise told the Beckers that April had contacted him to find out how to encourage communication with the entities there, and this alarmed him. Her relationship with her husband and children also began to deteriorate.

April then started to talk about "Henry". Was he one of the ghosts she had contacted on the Ouija board? She decided to hang out with seedy people; she became verbally abusive toward her husband and children. As time went by she became more violent to those around her, and the Beckers wondered if she was taking drugs. In the end, she ended up an unclaimed body in the Cook County morgue.

This true story illustrates how dangerous supernatural influences can unravel a person's life in stages. The entry point for these dark spirits was the communication and invitation extended to them.

HAUNTED TREASURES

The danger of hoarding extends from the physical to the metaphysical. Most of the people afflicted with this disorder are in denial and just call themselves collectors. A recent study found that between 5 to 14 million people in the United States are hoarders.

Medically it is defined as an excessive accumulation of things and the refusal to throw it away. The clutter can cause poor sanitation, eviction from a house or in severe cases; local code enforcement has no choice but to condemn a home. People living in these conditions are often afflicted with problems; financial, health, relationship and family.

The condition typically manifests in adolescence. Symptoms worsen in advanced age, when collected items have grown excessive and family members who would otherwise help to maintain and control the levels of clutter either die or move away.

Different people will hoard different items. Some collect "stuff", others bits of their own body, fingernails, strands of hair and urine. Others hoard animals.

Over 50 percent of hoarders suffer from other mental illnesses such as major depressive disorder, anxiety or social phobia.

How this ties into the paranormal is through two routes. First, a person living in these conditions have a certain level of chaos in their life. Some are able to disguise it and lead apparently normal lives, but that is not what is taking place for them emotionally and mentally. This chaotic undercurrent calls out to negative entities that thrive on this type of energy.

Clutter is arguably not part of feng shui, however it has the possibility to negatively impact the well-being of the occupant, by lowering the home's air quality and by bringing negative Qi.

The other way clutter allows negative paranormal encounters to enter your home is through items acquired at a thrift store, garages sales or curbside. In an earlier chapter, I advised to be careful about doing this and to systematically and metaphysically cleanse all items before they come into your home. However, if you are a hoarder you will take items home that you might not have room for, but more importantly disregarding any negative feel that comes from the item.

If the items belonged to a hoarder, they will cling more willfully than normal to even the most insignificant thing. This spirit might even lash out against the person that now has it, trying to establish ownership over their "precious". That is part of the hoarding process where even cheap "stuff" or trash will be considered treasure.

THE CURSED PRECIOUS THING

There are objects that become cursed, either intentionally by ritual or by the nature of the person who originally owned it.

The following is a story that played out almost a hundred years ago. It involves a ring that held a malicious curse that caused its successive owners to suffer injury, misfortune, even death.

It was 1920 and Hollywood had not produced "talkies" yet, but it had produced silent film heartthrobs. One of them was Rudolph Valentino.

One day Valentino saw a silver ring with a tiger's eye stone in a San Francisco curio shop. The owner told him it was called the Destiny Ring, and that he did not want to sell it because it was cursed. Whether he really did not want to sell it or he wanted to whet Valentino's appetite for the forbidden is unknown, but after that day, the ring had a new owner.

He wore it in his next film *The Young Rajah* (1922), which was a flop. He stopped wearing the ring until he was filming *Son of the Sheik* (1926) where he used it as a costume prop. This would be his last film.

Three weeks later, while touring in Manhattan to promote the film, he collapsed at the Hotel Ambassador suffering from appendicitis. He died on August 23 from peritonitis and pleuritis. He was thirty-one years old and he was wearing the ring.

The streets of Manhattan were thronged by an estimated 100,000 fans. There were reports of suicides over Valentino's unexpected death, including two women who tried to kill themselves in front of the hospital where he had died.

Actress Pola Negri, a Hollywood vamp who Valentino was romantically linked to became the next owner of the destiny ring. She collapsed at Valentino's funeral and she became seriously ill afterwards. Her career started sliding downwards after this event. In the next few months, she entered into a disastrous marriage and had a miscarriage.

She lived until she was 90, but perhaps she suspected the effect of the ring because she gave it away, despite claiming that Valentino had been the love of her life.

Eight years later, director Lansing Brown was planning a film about Rudy Valentino. He was considering using an actor and crooner named Russ Colombo to play Valentino in the movie.

Pola Negri was introduced to him, and she was so impressed by how much he looked like Valentino that she gave him the prized memento of her famous lover. This was something you think she would never have done considering its significance, unless her real intention was to put distance between herself and the ring. It did not take long before the ring claimed another victim.

It was September 1934 and Colombo was visiting Lansing Brown at his home. Brown mishandled an antique firearm he had in his collection, it went off, a ball ricocheted off a table and it embedded itself above Colombo's left eye.

He died a few hours later because of this freak accident. He was twenty-six years old and he had been using the ring.

Was it coincidental that Carol Lombard, Colombo's love interest, died in a plane crash in 1943?

The ring then went to gangster Joe Casino, a friend of Colombo. Casino was taking no chances with the curse, and he put the ring in a locked glass case. Whether he was convinced by friends not to be superstitious, or he thought the curse had worn off he started to wear the ring. Within a week, he was struck and killed by a truck.

The ring then went to Joe's brother, Del Casino. Very aware of the ring's reputation he did not even put it under glass; he stuck it in a safe.

In June 1938, director Eddie Small decided to make a film about Rudolph Valentino. He was considering an unknown actor named Jack Dunn to play the part. Dunn, 21, had followed his former skating partner turned actress, Sonja Henie to Hollywood. As part of his screen test, Small borrowed the ring from Del Casino so Dunn could wear it.

Jack was cast in the part, and allowed to keep the ring, which would be used during the actual filming.

Dunn's stroke of good luck was short-lived. In July, he was rushed to the hospital with a case of streptococcus infection. Within two weeks, he had died at Hollywood Hospital, a day before he was set to start shooting the Valentino film. His cause of death was a rare disease called tularemia, an infection spread by contact with wild rabbits. He had contracted this when he had been out hunting.

The ring was returned to Del Casino who promptly locked it away in his home. Oddly enough, Eddie Small was then considering casting Del Casino in his movie to play the part of Valentino. Eventually the movie plans were scrapped. Perhaps Del refused to wear the ring, no matter what.

Eventually Del wanted to distance the space between the ring and him even more, so he placed it in a vault in a Los Angeles bank.

Erroneously there is a report that a thief named James Willis stole the destiny ring from Del Casino. The truth of the matter is that in November 1940, Willis robbed a publicist named Beverly Barnett who was holding another ring that had belonged to Valentino, which was just a regular gold band. Inside it was inscribed "Rudolph Valentino 1924". It was part of the loot that was recovered by police after they shot Willis. Eventually Willis died from the gunshot wound.

In November 1939, the ring had been found in the dirt by actress Rochelle Hudson and her husband, while they were hiking in the area above Falcon's Lair, Valentino's former home in Benedict Canyon. While they were traveling, they left it with their publicist. Lucky for them it was stolen because it appears all of Valentino's jewelry was cursed.

Presently the exact whereabouts of Valentino's cursed "Destiny Ring" is unknown. Some believe it is still in the Los Angeles bank and is under the control of Del Casino's executors, others think it is not there any longer, based on a story, which appeared in a 1966 book authored by Chaw Mank and Brad Steiger titled *Valentino: An Intimate and Shocking Expose.*

In September 2017, a portrait of Valentino and Pola Negri wearing the cursed ring went up for sale. The painting was done by Federico Beltran Masses a month after Valentino's death; even then, the notoriety of the ring was well established.

The point of this story is that because the ring had belonged to Rudy Valentino it has been written about for several years. The origin of the jinx on this ring was never known. More obscure stories and trails of misfortune follow other objects that are never publicized. Many do end up locked away in vaults, others are in shops waiting for another "Rudy" to take it home with them. Do not be that person.

Rudolph Valentino + His Dog
c. Mid-1920s

Supernatural Safety

CRAZY FOR YOU

A deceased person who was troubled in life, whether due to mental illness and/or addiction and the problems that come with it, are attracted to living persons with similar problems. For example, they will be attracted to dysfunctional households where there is domestic violence and child abuse, similar to the environment they existed in while they were living.

The presence of this discarnate will drive a person to continue in risky behavior, despite their best attempts at stopping. Sometimes it will egg an individual on to abusive behavior towards those around them. How many times do these individuals ask themselves later, "why did I say that, why did I do that?"

Sometimes these entities are attracted to someone who they think is vulnerable for other reasons. What that translates into, is that they are aware this person might be influenced into behavior that will give them a chance to slip into their physical body to experience life, as they knew it. Remember this living person has something they desperately want, which is a human body with all its senses.

I had a case where a family had been experiencing minor paranormal phenomena for some years, but in the last months it had taken a violent and sinister tone. The family members had been experiencing nightmares, night visits, which they felt, had sexual overtones, and noises around the house especially around the windows and doors that faced the back of the property.

They had owned the house for forty years. Almost ten years before the wife had died in the house; she was suffering from cancer. The minor paranormal phenomena had been attributed to her, but the family felt guilty about trying to get her to leave.

The property had two sheds in the back. One held tools, the other that was larger; had been converted into a small efficiency. People who had stayed there had complained of noises underneath it and knockings at the windows.

The family, which was Catholic, was made up of the father and two other adults, his daughter and his niece. The client had approached his parish priest and asked for a house blessing. He told me that he could tell that the priest felt very uncomfortable, not with the house blessing part, but with his concerns that he had expressed about the haunting. He described where the priest had hurriedly done the blessing, told him he did not feel anything was amiss and quickly left. Unsurprisingly the activity increased after the priest's visit.

The client had reached out to a paranormal group for help, but since they could not respond right away, he asked a Santeria priest to try to expel whatever was there. He performed some type of ritual, which slowed things down but did not solve the problem.

The client's niece had tried to smudge the area outside of the house's windows in the back, and she had been chased away after suffering a severe case of vertigo.

I will not go into the details of the investigation, but I want to stress how important are the family dynamics and personalities of those living under the same roof. Especially how their past had to do with what was happening many years later.

Two ghosts were sensed there, one was undoubtedly the client's wife and another was a very dark human entity, which was causing much of the ominous phenomena.

The client then admitted that his wife in life had been a very jealous and possessive person. I asked him if she would have wanted him to stay unmarried, and he said yes. It appeared that the activity had started to ramp up almost a year before, when he started to think about getting romantically involved with another person.

He had retired four years before, but prior to that time he had had been working extended hours in order to maintain his household as a single parent, which left little room for romance.

We still could not figure out how this hostile, second male ghost had become attached to the property. The mystery was solved when he told us that his wife had been a nurse in a prison psychiatric ward for several years.

Later on, it was confirmed through psychic impressions that this entity had attached itself to the client's wife when she was living. Since she was deceased, there was no way to verify if she had any personality traits that aligned with this ghost, or if she was vulnerable in another way.

The client's decision to move on with his life, even though it was almost ten years after her death, had precipitated the manifestations from both of the entities.

We gave instructions on blessing the property and salting it down and invoking the help of St. Michael the Archangel in order to move his wife and the dark spirit attached to her on. The homeowner was urged to do the blessing himself. We also advised him that he had to work through his feelings of guilt in moving on with his life. This is not as simple as it sounds. This dynamic is not something logical, but emotional and you cannot snap your fingers and command yourself to feel differently about it.

As to the outcome of this case, it is better, though not resolved entirely.

The angle of this dark entity attaching to the client's wife when she was living, dovetails with the belief that ghosts may attach to a living person to suck the energy from them. Part of the energy drain can affect the person's immune system. Could this entity have brought about her death? No one will ever know.

THE POWER OF PROTECTION

This part concerns making sure you do not put the horse before the cart. Why, you may ask. In my experience, many people scramble for protection AFTER they have discovered that they are dealing with a dark haunting. Just think of the famous line from Forest Gump about the box of chocolates, well the paranormal is the same way, you never know what you are going to get. For this reason, you always prepare and make sure you are protected.

This is the first and most important part of a plan. Once you realize you might be dealing with something otherworldly, even if it turns out not to be the case, deciding to plan what to do next can return power to you. The importance of this cannot be overstated. Feeling powerless can increase fear; stagnation leads to frustration.

The one warning I can give you is not to let daylight dispel your intention to do something about any experience you had. If it occurred during the night, you might feel that what you saw or heard had a dreamlike quality. I have heard countless times about a person or entire families being in denial about unusual experiences they are having, and then realizing that procrastination did not solve the problem. Really analyze your experience and do not write it off as imagination if no other explanation applies.

When I get desperate calls asking me to respond immediately, the story usually starts with the phrase, "I thought it was my imagination", which is OK, but not if it has been going on for months or years.

The first step in a plan could be as easy as getting information. It could be a book like this one, internet research or even getting property records about where you live.

Sometimes people believe that rituals for protection have to be complicated, when in truth the simple approach can be very powerful. Knowledge is power.

INCENSE

The use of incense is found since ancient times. The first recorded instance was by the Egyptians approximately in 2400 B.C. It was also used for religious practices in China, Japan and other Asian civilizations. It was used in Christian Liturgy from its earliest centuries and was part of Jewish tradition before that. From passages found in the Bible it is inferred that incense was part of ritual cleansing and purification of sacred spaces.

The smoke of incense symbolizes sanctity and purity. It symbolizes prayers that rise to the Divine. It is an outward sign of spiritual realities.

Incense can allow stagnant energy that is stuck in your home to move freely. You can use any type but I prefer sage, frankincense and copal.

Sage is used for energy cleansing, especially to rid a space of negative energy. Sage is found in incense form and as smudge sticks. Palo Santo can also be used with it since it has a sweet aroma that can mask the overpowering scent of sage.

Frankincense can be used for protection, to ease feelings of stress. Copal has been considered sacred since ancient times and it can be paired with the frankincense.

You should cleanse your space during the daytime, and you can start by opening the doors to the home and the windows as well. Let in as much daylight as you can by pulling away any curtains or window coverings.

You can start by symbolically sweeping the front entrance to your home. You can either open cupboards, and closet doors ahead of time or as you go along. Face in from the front door, and start working clockwise if you are asking for protection; counter-clockwise if trying to dispel negative energy.

You can blow on an incense stick or smudge stick as you walk along, intoning, "Only light and love is allowed in this space, all negative energy and entities cannot exist here".

You can use any feather to spread the smoke before you as you walk along. Go to the corner of each room; open every closet door and cupboard of every room. This is especially important the first time you do this. You can do an abbreviated version as you do it consistently afterwards. Especially important is the attic and the basement, even if they are only used for storage.

Then salt the corners of each room since it works like a vacuum sucking up bad energy. Leave it there at least 48 hours before sweeping it away. Dispose of it outside in trash that is set to go out, or flush it down the toilet. If you have floors not carpet, mop using just a bit of ammonia that can be purchased with a lemon scent. Ammonia is also known as a ghost buster ingredient.

If you have a certain room where there is a lot of paranormal activity, or perhaps you notice, more arguments taking place there or even a sick room you can use this approach. Take any clear jar with a lid, fill it with spring water (that can be purchased at any grocery story), and add a pinch of salt and sage to it. Place a jar in the four corners of the room and then replace it within 24 hours. Just flush the water down the toilet.

You should couple this approach with whatever your spiritual or religious beliefs are. Again, I want to stress that the expectation that results are instantaneous can be a mistake. Many people stop because they do not see immediate results. Do not cheat yourself out of a solution because you want instant gratification.

I also believe in the power of aromatherapy. There is just something comforting and which in turn brings down stress levels, when the space you live in is clear of clutter and smells pleasant. This is part of the process of claiming the space as your sanctuary.

SOMEONE TO BELIEVE ME

These suggestions should be tailored to the situation you find yourself in, but the advice is to find someone you can confide in about what is happening to you. This can be family, friend or clergy. The two criteria you can use for this purpose is one, will this person believe you, and two, will this person keep your confidence if you ask them to.

Remind this person that when you tell them about what is going on, you are not necessarily asking them to supply a solution; all you want is a listening ear. Isolation is your enemy.

Do not forget that despite the reaction or disbelief from anyone else, you are still a powerful force that can make decisions and take action, especially if you are the adult in a household experiencing supernatural activity. You can also look at decisions that have to be made to protect your children or pets if they are being targeted.

There is nothing like being a defender to make you brave and resourceful. In the animal kingdom, there is no animal more dangerous than one defending its young, and after that its territory.

I suggest you should look for sources of positive energy. Go to a religious place, a park, a beach anywhere that uplifts your spirit and makes you happy. Initially you might think this is a waste of time, but the idea is to put time and distance between you and the source of your problem. A different setting allows you a different perspective. You do not telescope on how helpless and hopeless you feel. In fact, the idea is not to go there and think of your problems. This is a time where you disengage from trying to figure it out.

PRAYERS

The following are traditional prayers that can be amended to your religious beliefs, or whatever you feel is appropriate for your situation. If you believe that you are experiencing something paranormal, how can you not believe in the power of prayer?

Archangel Michael is the most revered of angels in Christian, Jewish and Islamic scriptures and tradition. This prayer was incorporated into the rubrics of the Low Mass of the Catholic Church from 1886 until its suppression in 1964.

> *Saint Michael Archangel, defend us in battle, be our protection against the wickedness and snares of the devil; may God rebuke him, we humbly pray; and do thou, O Prince of the heavenly host, by the power of God, cast into hell Satan and all the evil spirits who prowl through the world seeking the ruin of souls.*
> *[insert optional personal prayer here]. Amen*

Angel of God Prayer

> *Angel of God*
> *My guardian dear*
> *To Whom His love*
> *Commits me here*
> *Ever this day*
> *Be at my side*
> *To light and guard*
> *To rule and guide. Amen*

Violet Light Prayer (*This is based on the belief that a white light will actually attract discarnates to you. The violet light is just as protective*).

> *Father Sky, Mother Earth, put your violet light of love and protection around me, my home, my family and those that I love. Thank you for all your blessings. Take care of my animals and my property. I ask angels for the most benevolent outcome and to remind me to expect good things. As above, so below. I turn my life over to Divine Order. Everyday and everyway, I am getting better and better. Amen.*

Circle of Light

> *The light of God surrounds me.*
> *The love of God enfolds me.*
> *The power of God protects me.*
> *The presence of God watches over me.*

Wherever I am, God is.
And all is well.

Prayer of Confinement

In the name of Jesus Christ, I command all human spirits to be bound to the confines of the cemetery.
I command all inhuman spirits to go where Jesus Christ tells you to go, for it is He who commands you.
Amen

Exorcism of Salt
(Preparing Salt for Use in Driving Away Evil)

God's creature, salt, I cast out the demon from you by the living God, by the true God, by the holy God, by God who ordered you to be thrown into the waterspring by Eliseus to heal it of its barrenness. May you be a purified salt, a means of health for those who believe, a medicine for body and soul for all who make use of you. May all evil fancies of the foul fiend, his malice and cunning, be driven afar from the place where you are sprinkled. And let every unclean spirit be repulsed by Him who is coming to judge both the living and the dead and the world by fire.

Almighty everlasting God, we humbly appeal to your mercy and goodness to graciously bless this creature, salt, which you have given for mankind's use. May all who use it find in it a remedy for body and mind. And may everything that it touches or sprinkles be freed from uncleanness and any influence of the evil spirit; through Christ our Lord. Amen

Exorcism of water
(Preparing Water to be Used to Drive away Evil)

God's creature, water, I cast out the demon from you in the name of God the Father almighty, in the name of Jesus Christ, His Son, our Lord, and in the power of the Holy Spirit. May you be a purified water, empowered to drive afar all power of the enemy, in fact, to root out and banish the enemy himself, along with his fallen angels. We ask this through the power of our Lord Jesus Christ, who is coming to judge both the living and the dead and the world by fire.

O God, who for man's welfare established the most wonderful mysteries in the substance of water, hearken to our prayer, and pour forth your blessing on this element now being prepared with various purifying rites. May this creature of yours, when used in your mysteries and endowed with your grace, serve to cast out demons and to banish disease. May everything that this water sprinkles in the homes and gatherings of the faithful be delivered from all that is unclean and hurtful; let no breath of contagion hover there, no taint of corruption; let all the wiles of the lurking enemy come to nothing. By the sprinkling of this water may everything opposed to the safety and peace of the occupants of these homes be banished, so that in calling on your holy name they may know the well-being they desire, and be protected from every peril; through Christ our Lord. Amen.

<u>Preparing Holy Water with Salt</u>

Pour the salt into the water in the form of a cross, saying: May this salt and water be mixed together; in the name of the Father, and of the Son, and of the Holy Spirit.

God, source of irresistible might and king of an invincible realm, the ever-glorious conqueror; who restrain the force of the adversary, silencing the uproar of his rage, and valiantly subduing his wickedness; in awe and humility we beg you, Lord, to regard with favor this creature thing of salt and water, to let the light of your kindness shine upon it, and to hallow it with the dew of your mercy; so that wherever it is sprinkled and your holy name is invoked, every assault of the unclean spirit may be baffled, and all dread of the serpent's venom be cast out. To us who entreat your mercy grant that the Holy Spirit may be with us wherever we may be; through Christ our Lord. Amen.

Any of these prayers can be amended to your own preference, and to ask for the intercession dictated by your situation. There is no right or wrong prayers.

AMULETS, TALISMAN AND CHARMS

The word charm comes from the French word *charme*, which means song. The blessing that a priest gives at the end of a service is an example of this sort of charm.

Any item can be made into a charm by you. It could be a gift; it could also be something you found. Since the best use of a charm is something that you carry on your person, it is ideal if it is something small. It does not have to be visible, and it can be carried in a purse or under your clothing.

This old Irish rhyme explains why the four-leaf clover is considered a lucky charm:

> *One leaf is for fame,*
> *And one leaf is for wealth,*
> *And one is for a faithful lover,*

And one to bring you glorious health,
Are all in the four-leaved clover.

In his book *Amulets and Talismans for Beginners*, Richard Webster described how in 1968, contractors working on a project for the U.S. Navy blamed an absence of St. Christopher medals on the rockets for a succession of failures. Once the medal was added, the rockets performed without a hitch. The insistence on this particular saint is that he is the patron of the traveler and protects them while they are on the road.

Certain symbols can have both a religious and secular meaning. Fish presently symbolizes the Christian church, and at the same time, it is used as a charm to attract wealth and abundance.

Amulets are intended to be use as protection. They can be carried on your person; it can be drawn on a piece of paper, carved or made into a medal. The use of amulets is ancient.

In 1979, at an archeological site in Jerusalem adjacent to St. Andrew's Church, two tiny silver scrolls were found in caverns used as burial chambers. They were used as amulets and date back to the 7th century B.C. They became known as the Priestly Blessing, because they were rolled up and the priests would hang them around their neck. It contained passages from the book of Numbers 6:24-26.

The Lord bless you and keep you; the Lord make his face shine upon you and be gracious to you; the Lord turn his face toward you and give you peace.

Policemen are known to carry medals of St. Jude, which is the patron saint of law enforcement. However, amulets do not have to be of a person or animal. Knots can be used as amulets because they are believed to catch evil spirits. You can search for an amulet or wait for one to come to you.

Talismans are used to provide certain benefits. They can be inscribed with certain symbols, or a part of an animal such as a claw to gain the qualities you admire in it. It can also be a piece of clothing, like a "lucky" hat or pair of socks, which many athletes and fans are known to have as insurance that their team wins.

An easily recognizable talisman is the Seal of Solomon, which is made from two overlapping triangles. The one pointing down symbolizes water, earth and the feminine, the one pointing up stands for fire, sky and male energy.

Once you have chosen a talisman, you should make it your own. You can hold it and imagine a white, cleansing light around it, and then soak it overnight in a bowl of water and salt to remove the imprint of anyone who handled it before. Then leave it unused close by to your other possessions, or on a nightstand next to where you sleep. Do not let anyone else touch it. What you are doing is consecrating it to your use alone. Once you are ready to carry it with you, hold it in your hand and concentrate on what you want the talisman to do for you.

If you chose this talisman for a very specific use, once that is done, you can remove the talismanic intention by thanking it and either burning it, burying it or destroying it. Some people will keep a talisman for a lifetime.

CRYSTALS AND GEMS

Another aid that you can use to protect yourself or dispel negative energies is the use of crystals and gems.

My favorite pick and the one I have used for more than two decades is clear quartz crystal. They are inexpensive and are found around the world. They are very easy to program and resonate strongly with the eighth chakra that is known as the Seat of the Soul. It is the connection to the Divine Mind, and acts as a passage between your immortal soul and higher self. They are excellent for spiritual growth, and help you with any of the clair abilities.

The following four are very good for repelling evil and for protection. I have used them all at one time or another.

- Apache Tear - takes negative feelings such as grief and transforms it.
- Black Obsidian - works as protection against black magic and sorcery. It breaks ill fortune, spirit attachments and curses
- Black Tourmaline - this will protect your auric field and bounce back negative energy.
- Labradorite - shields you against psychic attacks and for those who can create negative thought forms because they obsess about ways to wish you ill.

Periodically you should cleanse and recharge your crystals. Just run them under clear water and leave them outside where the sun hits them, or if at night wait until the full moon is out. I do this exercise every four to six weeks, but more often if I use them in an investigation. My crystals go with me everywhere in a pouch inside my purse.

THE POWER OF THE BELL

There is a theory that bells have power over the supernatural and their sounds can drive away demons.

Bells would be baptized and blessed with psalms, salt and holy water in order to consecrate them to the use of a particular church.

Bells have been part of divine worship and is preserved in the *Roman Ritual* blessing of bells that reads, "at its sound let all evil spirits be driven afar". You can buy a small handbell for this purpose. I found a small, silver-tone one with a Christmas motif at a thrift store. It was very inexpensive.

This tool is the equivalent of a cattle prod and raking your nails on the chalkboard for unwanted entities in your home.

FOLKLORE AND FAIRYTALES

Some of the following suggestions you can categorize as folklore or fairytale, but in many cases, they are found across different cultures and beliefs, which indicate some kernel of truth in them.

There is a belief that certain colors protect or act as a deterrent against ghosts. One of them is a pale blue-green tint known as "haint blue". This so-called haunted blue color represented the color of water, which a spirit cannot cross. Ceilings, window trim, porches and doors are painted in this color in order to act as a barrier.

While visiting Charleston a few years ago, I saw exterior window trim painted in this color on several structures. A local person who was in the group confirmed that this was called "haint blue". The person told me that it was intentionally used to ward off spirits. It was no coincidence that these houses were close to the old Charleston Jail, which had a reputation of being very haunted. It was in use from 1802 to 1939.

Belief in the power of this blue green color dates back to ancient Greece, where the people would use jewelry and body decorations made of lapis lazuli, which mimics the cyan color. The ancient Egyptians also used this color. The same color is used to ward off the "evil eye". Blue stones mounted on gold and silver are presented to babies and small children as a talisman for protection.

Muslims call it the Hand of Fatima, while Jews refer to it as the Hand of Miriam, hamsa hand or hamesh hand. Both faiths, however, agree on its powers. The hand with the colored eye will shield you from the powers of the evil eye.

Perhaps the origins of this belief started with the ancient Egyptians who would line their eyes heavily, believing that the smoky makeup would prevent evil from entering through their eyes. Obviously, the

Egyptians believed that the eyes are the windows of the soul.

Most people are familiar with the belief that garlic has the power to repel vampires, however it can protect from psychic vampires as well. Carrying garlic when sailing on a boat is believed to protect against drowning or the boat sinking. Roman soldiers would carry it into battle since it was thought to bring courage. Knights during medieval times believed it protected them against their enemies.

In Chinese belief, the world is populated by both good and bad spirits. The evil ones are believed to shun light and to be able to travel only in straight lines, thus many roads in China are curvy.

They make a distinction between an evil spirit and an unhappy one. Unhappy ghosts might be ancestors who died violently, were not buried properly or have no family members to remember and honor them.

If you would like to symbolically use the power of light, you can burn a small, white votive candle when you say prayers or any other effort to banish a ghost in your home. This should be an unused candle, or what is known as a "virgin candle". Do not use a match to light the candle as the sulfur will banish your intent, and do not blow out the candle for the same reason. What this means is that you should light the candle when you know you can stay home and keep a vigil on it until it burns down.

The Japanese call the northeast corner (45 degrees on the compass) of a room "kimon", which means demon's gate or the outer gate. They see it as the entry point for bad spirits, which is why you should never hang any mirrors on either wall at that convergence point.

If this is a bedroom, it should not be used by children, or adults who are suffering from an illness. If possible, this room should be used as a storage room, and if not to leave at least this corner empty.

The same holds true for any bedroom in a straight line from this point (215 degrees on the compass) which is the inner gate of the spiritual realm.

The Power of Iron

Iron has a reputation that it can repel, bind or harm ghosts, witches, fairies and other malevolent entities.

This dates back to ancient Egypt and the evil god-demon Set or Typhon as he was known by the Greeks. Iron was known as the Bones of Typhon. The power of iron is based on fighting fire with fire.

This is why horseshoes are nailed over doors and cemeteries are surrounded by iron fences in order to contain the souls of the dead. Burying an iron knife under the entrance to your home will keep humans under the control of evil or malevolent beings from entering.

CHAPTER 5
WHERE THE RUBBER MEETS THE ROAD

This is the moment when you execute what you have been planning. When I say "you" this is a collective you that could include your spouse, your children or anyone else in your household that is being affected by paranormal phenomena.

This is when I suggest you sit down and write out a short summary of what you have experienced that you think is paranormal.

Right about now I am hearing a groan from the non-writers. When I say write, it could be a few words per line; it does not have to be an essay.

Then write down names, phone numbers, emails or website addresses for sources that you have come across that you are going to use. Even if you have this information in your phone or on your computer, I would urge you to write it out. The reason why I suggest this, is that the supernatural has a peculiar, but very effective method of sabotaging your efforts to access all the information you have gathered; from power outages to actually freezing your phone or crashing your computer.

Include any information you have researched along the way. Remember this is your command post, your go to point to handle what is going on. Even if you have a paranormal team or clergy coming in to help you, at the end of the day you are the one that will be staying to live there and you are not going to let up on your assault on whatever is there.

Add anything you think is important because you are about to do it! What are you going to do? You are going to EXECUTE!

This is when you start implementing whatever you have decided to do. You can only research so much before you move on even without a guarantee of success. This is when you have to have faith.

Depending on your religious or spiritual beliefs, if you are going to pray, do it aloud. Use the power of your voice. You do not have to shout, just say it in a normal voice.

I would say that the most important practice you can incorporate into your approach to resolve supernatural events in your home, is consistency. Do not be intimidated if things ramp up, and do not become complacent if it appears everything is back to normal.

I recommend addressing the deceased in your home on a daily basis. You are going to remind them repeatedly about the obvious which is that they are dead. You also urge them to go into the light. Remind them that this is your house now, and that you do not want them there. Be firm, but not angry or antagonistic.

This is one part where other paranormal researchers and I diverge. I do not believe in being friends with ghosts and leaving them to stay in the house. I will repeat what I said at the beginning of the book, this usually ends badly for the humans living there. It might take years, but make no mistake it will arrive at that point where the living will ask themselves how they let things get so bad. Eventually many families feel they are in over their head and just move out, even if otherwise they would stay in a home they love.

The reasons for my precaution in not letting a ghost stay are the following: one, the entity is masquerading to buy itself more time to stay among the living. When I say masquerading, it will appear helpless, as either a child or woman or an older person. The other situation is that even if the entity is just a sad, confused human spirit, it will eventually grow frustrated and angry because it will see human beings living out their lives, something they cannot do. No matter what!

LET US DO IT THE HARD WAY

If the paranormal events happening to you or in your home originated from a residual haunting, or a confused soul you will see the activity start to decline or space out as you implement any plans you have decided to use.

In some cases, a ghost will resist your efforts, or go to the next step of trying to scare you into stopping by retaliating. This does not mean your approach was wrong, sometimes it means quite the opposite.

Perhaps you had a layered haunting, which means the human souls were moved on and what is left are non-human entities, which had been using the others as decoys.

The manifestations might become more violent, and your first consideration should be children and pets in the home that could be hurt.

The haunting could take a malicious and unpredictable turn. The reason for this is that the entity is hoping to scare you off, and that you will stop your efforts or move out.

Some human entities will resist removal and demonstrate very disturbing manifestations. These might be the ghosts of someone with some type of mental illness when they were alive. Since they are stuck in the death state, they still suffer from the illness.

Many homeowners make the mistake of attempting spirit communication at this point, whether through automatic writing, a Ouija board or any other device in hopes of discovering who or what is there.

This should only be done by a seasoned and experienced medium that can convince a ghost to move on, and possibly reassure it that all the answers, love and forgiveness they seek can be found in the light. The medium can also verify if indeed the haunting is linked to a non-human or demonic entity.

If one of the homeowners starts to do this, even if it is running a recorder to capture an EVP you are undoing any progress you have made. Just imagine you have gotten an intruder out of your home, they are still on your porch trying to gain entry and you open the door a little bit and start a dialogue by asking, "What do you want?" The entity has essentially gotten their foot in the door again. How much easier do you think it is for an intruder to push himself back into your home at this stage?

To show mercy and compassion to a human soul who is still clinging to this plane, is best done by praying for them and asking angels and other enlightened spirits to come and convince them to go into the light.

If it is a non-human entity, you ask for angelic help as well. These beings are on an equal footing with whatever is there, and in truth, they are superior to it. Something very important to remember here is that these angels cannot help you until you ask for it. All you have to do is ask for protection, and for this entity to be taken to the most appropriate place. There are places, where us as living beings, cannot conceive or know of.

Chapter 6
When to Call in the Calvary

The decision to call in a paranormal team or a medium might be done right at the beginning, or after you have tried certain measures and they have not worked. If you or someone in your family is being terrorized physically and/or psychologically, then most certainly reach out for help.

When contacting a paranormal team I urge you to do a little bit of research, and seek one out that has been established a few years, the longer the better. The member you are looking for that is been there the longest, is the founder.

A good majority of paranormal teams dissolve within the first or second year, so when you find a team that has several years under its belt, you are probably dealing with at least some members who actually have field experience in dealing with a haunting. By this I mean, they do not have knowledge based on a book or watching a paranormal reality show. They have hands on, field experience.

FIRST INTERVIEW

The majority of paranormal teams have a website that you can look over, and see pictures of their members and of past investigations. In my experience, the majority of sites are a little bit outdated, or many of their cases do not appear there because of privacy reasons.

Usually the contact starts with an email. Do not be tempted to write out everything that is going on in the email, because in truth you want to gauge first if this is the team you want to work with. Once you get a phone call, you can ask questions as well as fill in the person who is calling about what has been happening.

There are two things you should be on the lookout for. One is a genuine interest in helping you and the other if there is any cost involved. Some teams appreciate a donation towards gasoline if they are traveling a distance to help you, but it is not a deal breaker if you cannot offer them any money.

I suggest you have a list of questions already written up to ask them. Some important points to touch on are: how much experience they have, how many members will be coming, what type of equipment will they be using, will they share their findings with you on a written report, and finally can they help you if this turns out to be a dark haunting. You might ask yourself if this is getting ahead of the outcome of the investigation, but it would not be the first time I have heard of teams coming in, identifying the source and then leaving, especially if it turns out to have a malevolent twist to it. Some teams will have a member of clergy that will come in to help if this is what it turns out to be, but this should be something you want to know about ahead of time, when deciding who to use.

Do not be put off if you contact a team that has very few members, but they are all well experienced. Some of the best teams I know of usually have a small group of researchers, who are hardcore investigators. These are what I call A-team ghost hunters who have shed wannabe, weekend thrill seekers and have handled a wide range of cases.

Most teams have a psychic or sensitive as part of their team, and others have access to a medium. This psychic can communicate with the dead. Not all psychics can do this. Some teams might have to schedule a second visit in order to come back with a medium.

In the end, if you do not feel comfortable or confident with whom you are speaking to, do not be afraid to keep looking for another team. Remember as much as you need help, you are also going to be opening your home to strangers.

POST INVESTIGATION

My advice is to keep up a regular ritual of using salt and any other methods you were employing before; at least once per month if not more often. Smudging is also very helpful, because even though the ghosts are gone from the place you want to keep good energy flowing throughout the space.

It is usual to be a little jumpy after an investigation. You think every noise is the return of whatever was sent on its way, and you will have to make an effort to push down the fear. As the days go by this will become easier and easier. Remember fear makes you weak and the one who was out of place was the ghost, not you.

Another feeling you have to avoid is guilt. Sometimes people feel like they have shoved a human being, even if it just a ghost, out into the cold, cruel world of the beyond. In truth, when you have helped a ghost to cross over, or to be taken a few steps closer to the light you are performing spirit rescue.

You are helping to pull a human spirit away from the attraction of a world it no longer belongs to. These anchors sometime tethers a ghost for years locked in bitterness, frustration and confusion.

Once it is no longer tied to its existence as a living thing, it is more apt to pay attention to the bright light where it should have gone originally. It will hear the voice of angels and loved once who preceded them there.

Even though you might never be aware of it, heaven will thank you for your actions.

If it was an inhuman entity when you asked for intercession from beings who are charged to do this work, you are committing an action to one of the most important things a human being (a live one that is) can do, which is self-preservation.

In closing, do not lose faith in your ability and power to cleanse and protect the place where you choose to live. Your home is your sanctuary, both physically and spiritually, the place where you and your family should feel safe.

Sources

Becker, E. (2015). *True haunting 2*. New Jersey: BookBaby.

Fodor, N. (1959). *The haunted mind*. New York: Helix Press

Foster, B. M., & Foster, M. (2002). *The secret lives of Alexandra David-Neel: A biography of the explorer of Tibet and its forbidden practices*. Woodstock, NY: Overlook

Godfrey, L. S. (2016). *Monsters among us: an exploration of otherworldly bigfoots, wolfmen, portals, phantoms, and odd phenomena*. New York: TarcherPerigee

Johnson, B. (2007). Black Hope horror does not haunt this hood. Retrieved from https://www.chron.com/neighborhood/article/Black-Hope-horror-doesn-t-haunt-this-hood-9565799.php

Koontz, D. (2007). *Brother Odd*. New York: Bantam

Marryat, F. (2004). *There is no death*. New York: Cosimo Classics.

Roll, W. (1972). *The poltergeist*. New York: Signet

Webster, R. (2017). *Amulets and talismans for beginners - how to choose, make and use magical objects.* Woodbury: Llewellyn Publications.

Williams, B., Williams, J. and Shoemaker, J. (1993). *The black hope horror.* New York: Berkley Books.

(n.d.). Retrieved from https://www.sanctamissa.org/en/resources/books-1962/rituale-romanum/48-blessings-for-special-days-and-feasts.html

<u>Newspapers and Periodicals</u>

The Miami News
The Lakeland Ledger
The San Francisco Examiner
The Examiner
The Tribune
The Los Angeles Times

www.ingramcontent.com/pod-product-compliance
Lightning Source LLC
Chambersburg PA
CBHW051342040426
42453CB00007B/376